Plastics and Polymers Science Fair Projects

Acknowledgments
The author thanks Valerie A. Wilcox, Executive Director of the National Plastics Center and Museum, for arranging a guided tour, and Anne-Marie Arnold, In-House Education Director, for giving the tour of the museum.

Library of Congress Cataloging-in-Publication Data

Goodstein, Madeline P.
  Plastics and polymers science fair projects, revised and expanded using the scientific method / by Madeline Goodstein.
    p. cm. — (Chemistry science projects using the scientific method)
  Summary: "Explains how to use the scientific method to conduct several science experiments with plastics and polymers. Includes ideas for science fair projects"—Provided by publisher.
  Includes bibliographical references and index.
  ISBN-13: 978-0-7660-3412-9
  ISBN-10: 0-7660-3412-7
  1. Polymers—Experiments—Juvenile literature. 2. Plastics—Experiments—Juvenile literature. 3. Science projects—Juvenile literature. I. Title.
  QD381.3.G659 2010
  540.78—dc22
                            2008046504

Printed in the United States of America

092009 Lake Book Manufacturing, Inc., Melrose Park, IL

10 9 8 7 6 5 4 3 2 1

♻ Enslow Publishers, Inc. is committed to printing our books on recycled paper. The paper in every book contains between 10% to 30% post-consumer waste (PCW). The cover board on the outside of each book contains 100% PCW. Our goal is to do our part to help young people and the environment too!

Illustration Credits: Tom LaBaff and Stephanie LaBaff

Editorial Revision: Lily Book Productions

Design: Oxygen Design

Photo Credits: Clint Hild/iStockphoto.com, p. 3; Shutterstock, pp. 6, 32, 98, 126; courtesy of Mr. Christopher V. Kelly and Professor Mark M. Banaszak Holl, University of Michigan, p. 60.

Cover Photos: Shutterstock

Revised edition of *Plastics and Polymers Science Fair Projects Using Hair Gel, Soda Bottles, and Slimy Stuff,* Copyright © 2004.

Chemistry Science Projects
Using the Scientific Method

Plastics and Polymers Science Fair Projects

Revised and Expanded
Using the Scientific Method

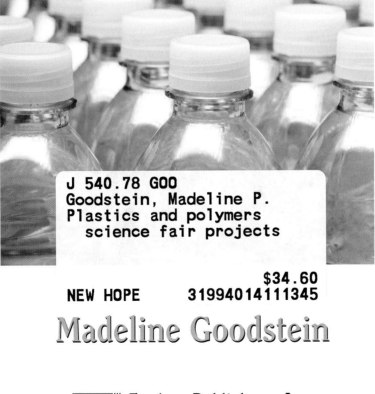

Madeline Goodstein

Enslow Publishers, Inc.
40 Industrial Road
Box 398
Berkeley Heights, NJ 07922
USA
http://www.enslow.com

Contents

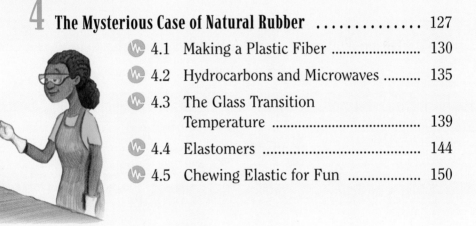
 Indicates experiments that contain Science Project Ideas.

INTRODUCTION

Plastics and Polymers Experiments and Projects Using the Scientific Method

What comes to mind when you think of plastics? How about wash-and-wear clothing that doesn't need ironing; bicycle and motorcycle helmets that save lives; thin, clear wrap to keep food moist and safe; automobile tires good for sixty thousand miles; bullet-proof vests; picnic cups that keep hot drinks hot and cold drinks cold; glue so "instant" that you have to be careful not to glue your fingers together; CDs and cassettes with your favorite music; carpets where food spills can be washed right off; and pot handles, quick-drying paints, chair and couch upholstery, airplane windows, tabletops and countertops, foam mattresses,

◄ Protected by a helmet and goggles made of plastics, a freestyle motocross competitor performs a daring stunt.

patio chairs, boat hulls, vinyl floor tiles, dishes, toys, bathtub caulk, plumbing pipes, fences, insulation, surgical gowns, computer chips, and much more. As you can see, plastics are used for many things in our lives.

How do you know when something is plastic? Often, you can tell that something is plastic when you lift it. This is because many plastics are lightweight. The feel of the plastic is often another way to tell. A chunk of plastic feels firm yet not as hard as metal. Plastic wraps have their own special properties. They are soft and flexible. A plastic wrap sticks to itself and can be stretched.

Weight, feel, and stretchability are all special characteristics of plastics that are unlike those of other materials. Why do plastics have these properties? The answers to this question will be explored in the experiments in this book.

What Are Plastics and Polymers?

What is a plastic? What makes it different from other materials? The answer is a chemical one. All plastics are made of a special kind of chemical. This special kind of chemical is called a polymer. Plastics are all made principally of polymers. A polymer is a very large molecule. A polymer molecule may be thousands or even millions of times larger than a non-polymer molecule.

For any substance, the smallest bit of matter that can be identified as that substance is called a molecule. An example of a molecule that we all know is the water molecule, H_2O. The tiny particles that together make up a cup or a pond or a lake of water are each made up of two hydrogen (H) atoms and one oxygen (O) atom. Each H_2O particle is a molecule, the smallest bit of water possible.

Until polymers were discovered, it was believed that all molecules were made up of small numbers of atoms. The discovery of polymers changed that belief. Now, we know that polymer molecules are made up of hundreds, thousands, or even hundreds of thousands of atoms in long chains or networks (chains connected to each other at various spots).

Does the extreme length of the polymer molecule give it properties very different from that of small molecules? The answer to that is a resounding *yes*! The length of a polymer molecule accounts for the distinctive behaviors of the plastics they make.

The long chains are formed from small molecules called monomers. Monomers combine end to end in a chemical reaction to form the polymer chain. Imagine a group of identical boys gathered in a school gymnasium: Figure 1a. When a signal is given, the boys all have to join hands in a long chain as shown in Figure 1b. The long chain is the polymer. Each boy is a monomer. The process of polymer formation from monomers is called polymerization. Many chains may be formed at the same time, and the chains may even join together to form a network.

Figure 1.

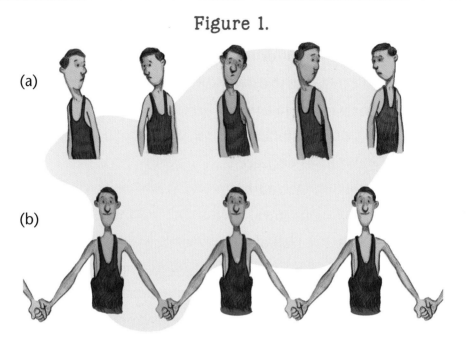

(a)

(b)

a) In this model, each boy represents a monomer.
b) When the boys join hands, they form a polymer.

A polymer may also form from two different monomers. For example, the gymnasium might hold a large number of boys and girls. At a signal, one boy is required to clasp a girl's hand. Holding on to the first boy, the girl clasps the hand of another boy with her other hand. Holding on, that boy clasps another girl's hand and so on until a long chain is formed. The boys and girls represent monomers that bond together to form the repeat segment. The chain of repeat segments is a polymer, as shown in Figure 2. Again, many chains may form, and they may join together to form a network.

All of the wonderful man-made plastic products that improve our lives today are based on polymers. Usually, plastics contain more than just the polymer or polymers.

Additives are introduced to make the polymer more flexible or more heat-resistant or to improve whatever special quality is needed to make it useful.

If all the plastics in the world suddenly disappeared, you might find yourself standing naked on a dirt floor. If all the natural polymers disappeared, you wouldn't exist! Proteins, certain sugars, DNA, and RNA—all of which help to make up our bodies—are natural polymers. Plants would not exist either, because the wall of a plant cell is built of cellulose, a natural polymer. The starch that helps to make up plants is also a natural polymer.

This book has many experiments designed to illustrate how the length and structure of a polymer chain cause it to have special properties. By doing these experiments, you can get started learning about what causes gooey, bouncy, stretchy, rubbery, hard, flexible, or glassy plastics.

Figure 2.

In this model of a polymer, each boy represents one specific monomer and each girl stands for a different monomer. The "monomers" join together in a chemical reaction to form a boy-girl sequence that repeats for the entire length of the "polymer" chain. A combination of boy-girl-girl would produce a different polymer.

Advantages of Plastics

Why have polymers become so widely used? In less than a century, they have replaced wood, metal, marble, fabric, paint, caulking, glue, and other products in many places. A major reason for their popularity is that plastics are easy to shape. Polymers can be molded into desired forms, drawn into fibers (threads), stretched, and/or bent. Also, the raw materials that make them are easy to obtain and often inexpensive. Plastics are usually lightweight and not damaged by chemicals. Many polymers are waterproof. Some plastics are such good electrical insulators that they are used to coat electrical wiring. It is no wonder there are so many uses for plastics.

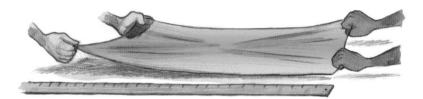

Experiments and Projects

This book contains lots of fun experiments about polymers and plastics. You will also be given suggestions for independent investigations that you can do yourself. Most of the experiments are followed by a section called Science Project Ideas. This section contains great ideas for your own science fair projects.

All the materials needed for the experiments in this book are available in your home, or at the supermarket, hardware store, or drug store. Many experiments use only small quantities of materials. As a result, you may often be able to obtain them at no cost from people already using them. For example, you might ask a plumber for some epoxy putty or a painter for some solvents. Your school science teacher may occasionally be able to help you obtain some of the materials needed and may also be able to offer you guidance on projects.

The experiments in this book are all easy to do and safe to carry out when the instructions are followed as given. Consult with your school science teacher or some **other responsible adult** to obtain approval before starting any experiments of your own.

There may be some words involving plastics in this book that are new and unfamiliar to you. These terms are included in the glossary.

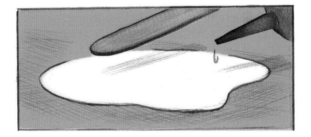

How Scientists Search for Answers

When scientists have a question to answer, they start by researching. They read scientific literature and consult online science databases that are maintained by universities, research centers, or the government. There, they can study abstracts—summaries of reports—by scientists who have conducted experiments or have done similar research in the field.

In this way, they find out whether other scientists have examined the same question or have tried to answer it by doing an

experiment. Careful research will tell what kind of experiments, if any, have been done to try to answer the question.

Scientists don't want to repeat experiments that have known and accepted outcomes. Also, they want to avoid repeating any mistakes others may have made while doing similar experiments. If no one else has done scientific work that answers their question, scientists then do further research on how best to do the experiment.

While researching for the experiment, the scientist tries to guess—or predict—the possible results. This prediction is called a hypothesis.

The scientist hopes that a well-researched and carefully planned experiment will prove the hypothesis to be true. At times, however, the results of even the best-planned experiment can be far different from what the scientist expected. Yet even if the results indicate the hypothesis was not true, this does not mean the experiment was a failure. In fact, unexpected results can provide valuable information that leads to a different answer or to another, even better, experiment.

Using the Scientific Method in Experiments and Projects

The Scientific Method

A scientific experiment starts when someone wonders what would happen if certain conditions were set up and tested by following a specific process.

For example, what if the temperature at which a certain polymer experiment took place is increased? A guess about what would happen is called your hypothesis. Some possible hypotheses might be:

✓ The polymer formed will become stiffer.
✓ Less of the polymer will form.
✓ The polymer will turn dark.

Let's say your hypothesis is that less of the polymer will form as the temperature is increased.

For a start, we have to know that a scientific experiment has only two variables—that is, only two things that can change. For this experiment, one variable would be the temperature at which the experiment takes place, and the other would be the amount of the polymer formed.

Nothing else is allowed to change, not the quantities of the reacting materials, or the time allowed for the reaction to take place, or even what the reaction container is made of. This is because if anything else besides the two variables were allowed to change, it would not be possible to tell what had caused the change in the quantity of polymer formed.

Now, if the experiment is carried out and no change in the quantity of polymer is observed, it would not mean that the experiment is a failure. Even if your hypothesis that less of the polymer will form as the temperature is increased turns out to be false, all results—positive or negative—provide important information. The results can lead to further ideas that can be explored.

In this book, you will be conducting scientific experiments. The results of these experiments and the conclusions you reach may lead to new experiments that you can carry out for yourself.

Scientists may develop logical explanations for the results of their experiments. These explanations, or theories, must be tested by more experiments. If the resulting data from experiments provide compelling support for a theory, the theory could be accepted by the world of science. But scientists are careful about accepting new theories. If any of the experimental results contradict a theory, then the theory must be discarded, altered, or retested. That is the scientific method.

Basic Steps in the Scientific Method

The best experiments and science projects usually follow the scientific method's basic steps:

- ✓ Ask questions about what would happen if certain conditions or events were set up and tested in an experiment.

- ✓ Do background research to investigate the subject of your question.

- ✓ Construct a hypothesis—an answer to your question—that you can then test and investigate with an experiment.

- ✓ Design and conduct an experiment to test your hypothesis.

- ✓ Keep records, collect data, and then analyze what you've recorded.

- ✓ Draw a conclusion based on the experiment and the data you've recorded.

- ✓ Write a report about your results.

Your Hypothesis

Many experiments and science projects begin by asking whether something can be done or how it can be done. In this book's experiment "Making Slime: Cross-Linking," the question is, "Can separate chains of polymer molecules link together and form a solid?"

The educated guess (the hypothesis) that answers the question is, "The polymer in glue can cross–link and make polymer chains. The resulting slimy substance can be kneaded into a plastic ball."

How do you test this hypothesis? First you should study how chemical reactions can change one substance into another. Some background research into the process of polymer "cross-linking" will prepare you to understand the complex chemical processes behind a simple experiment—making slime, or putty.

You should find out what methods, chemicals, and polymers are needed to design an experiment that will test your hypothesis. By using the right tools and materials—in this case white glue, borax, and an ordinary jar and cup—you can cause the important polymer reaction called "cross-linking" to take place.

Remember: To give your experiment or project every chance of success, prepare a hypothesis that is clear and brief. The simpler the better.

Designing the Experiment

Your experiment will be structured to investigate whether the hypothesis is true or false. The experiment is intended to test the hypothesis, not necessarily to prove that the hypothesis is right.

The results of a well-designed experiment are more valuable than the results of an experiment that is intentionally designed to give the answer you want. The conditions you set up in your experiment must be a fair test of your hypothesis. For example, in the cross-linking experiment you should follow the instructions carefully when adding water to the borax solution in order to allow it to mix properly with the white glue. And when you add more borax to the mix, observe how this affects the slime. By paying attention to what happens when different quantities of borax are used, you'll discover key information that can be recorded as data (observations).

It is most important that the experiment's procedures and results are as accurate as possible. Design the experiment for observable, measurable results. And keep it simple, because the more complicated your experiment is, the more chance you have for error.

Also, if you have friends helping you with an experiment or project, make sure from the start that they will take their tasks seriously.

Remember: Scientists around the world always use metric measurements in their experiments and projects, and so should you. Use metric liquid and dry measures and a Celsius thermometer.

Recording Data

Your hypothesis, procedure, data, and conclusions should be recorded immediately as you experiment, but don't keep it on loose scraps of paper. Record your data in a notebook or logbook—one you use just for experiments. Your notebook should be bound so that you have a permanent record. The laboratory notebook is an essential part of all academic and scientific research.

Make sure to include the date, experiment number, and a brief description of how you collected the data. Write clearly. If you have to cross something out, do it with just a single line, then rewrite the correct information.

Repeat your experiment several times to be sure your results are consistent and your data are trustworthy. Don't try to interpret data as you go along. It's better first to record results accurately, then study them later.

You might even find you want to replace your experiment's original question with a new one. For example, "Can separate chains of polymer molecules link together and form a solid?" brings up a broader question: "Why do different types of cross-linked chains of polymers often react differently when they're stretched, squeezed, or bounced?"

Writing the Science Fair Report

Communicate the results of your experiment by writing a clear report. Even the most successful experiment loses its value if the scientist cannot clearly tell what happened. Your report should describe how the experiment was designed and conducted and should state its precise results.

Following are the parts of a science fair report, in the order they should appear:

• The Title Page
The title of your experiment should be centered and near the top of the page. Your teacher will tell you what other information is needed, such as your name, grade, and the name of your science teacher.

• Table of Contents
On the report's second page, list the remaining parts of the report and their page numbers.

• Abstract

Give a brief overview of your experiment. In just a few sentences, tell the purpose of the experiment, what you did, and what you found out. Always write in plain, clear language.

• Introduction

State your hypothesis and explain how you came up with it. Discuss your experiment's main question and how your research led to the hypothesis. Tell what you hoped to achieve when you started the experiment.

• Experiment and Data

This is a detailed step-by-step explanation of how you organized and carried out the experiment. Explain what methods you followed and what materials and equipment you used.

State when the experiment was done (the date, perhaps the time of day, too) and under what conditions (in a laboratory, outside on a windy day, in cold or warm weather, etc.) Tell who was involved and what part they played in the experiment. Include clearly labeled graphs and tables of data from the experiment as well as any photographs or drawings that help illustrate your work. Anyone who reads your report should be able to repeat the experiment just the way you did it. (Repeating an experiment is a good way to test whether the original results were obtained correctly.)

• Discussion

Explain your results and conclusions, perhaps comparing them with published scientific data you first read about in your research. Consider how the experiment's results relate to your hypothesis. Ask yourself: Do my results support or contradict my hypothesis? Then analyze the answer.

Would you do anything differently if you did this experiment again? State what you've learned as a result of the experiment.

Analyze how your tools and equipment did their tasks, and how well you and others used those tools. If you think the experiment could be done better if designed another way or if you have another hypothesis that might be tested, then include this in your discussion.

• Conclusion

Make a brief summary of your experiment's results. Include only information and data already stated in the report, and be sure not to bring in any new information.

• Acknowledgments

Give credit to everyone who helped you with the experiment. State the names of these individuals and briefly explain who they are and how they assisted you.

• References / Bibliography

List any books, magazines, journals, articles, Web sites, scientific databases, and interviews that were important to your research for the experiment.

Science Fairs

Most experiments and projects in this book are followed by Science Project Ideas. This section has great ideas for your science fair project. However, judges at such fairs don't reward projects or experiments that are simply copied from a book. And it doesn't impress judges if your project is too easy: for instance if you just compared the stretchability of the plastics Silly Putty and Slime. If, however, you made your own plastic putty and compared all three, then judges would likely give you serious consideration.

You could record additional factors, such as: Do Silly Putty and Slime flow when placed on a vertical surface? Do they pick up ink from printed paper? What properties do they have that your homemade putty doesn't have? What happens when you add different ingredients to yours?

Science fair judges tend to reward creative thought and imagination. It is difficult to be creative or imaginative unless you are really interested in your project, so be sure to choose a subject that appeals to you. And before you jump into a project, consider, too, your own talents and the cost of materials you will need.

If you decide to use a project found in this book for a science fair, you should find ways to modify or extend it. This should not be difficult because you'll probably discover that, as you do these projects, new ideas for experiments will come to mind—experiments that could make excellent science fair projects, particularly because the ideas are your own and are interesting to you.

If you decide to enter a science fair and have never done so before, you should read some of the books listed in the Further Reading section. The books with titles that refer to science fairs will provide plenty of helpful hints and information that will enable you to avoid the pitfalls that sometimes plague first-time entrants. You will learn how to prepare appealing reports that include charts and graphs, how to set up and display your work, how to present your project, and how to relate to judges and visitors.

Following are some suggestions to consider.

Some Tips for Success at a Science Fair

Science teachers and science fair judges have many different opinions on what makes a good science fair project or experiment. Here are the most important elements:

Originality of Concept is one of the most important things judges consider. Some judges believe that the best science fair projects answer a question that isn't found in a science textbook.

Scientific Content is another main area of evaluation. How was science applied in the procedure? Are there sufficient data? Did you stick to your intended procedure and keep good records?

Thoroughness is next in importance. Was the experiment repeated as often as needed to test your hypothesis? Is your notebook complete, and are the data accurate? Does your research bibliography show you did enough library work?

Clarity in how you present your exhibit shows you had a good understanding of the subject you worked on. It is important that your exhibit clearly presents the results of your work.

Effective Process: Judges recognize that how skillfully you carry out a science fair project is usually more important than its results. A well-done project gives students the best understanding of what scientists actually do day-to-day.

Other points to consider when preparing for your science fair:

The Abstract: Write up a brief explanation of your project and make copies for visitors or judges who want to read it.

Knowledge: Be ready to answer questions from visitors and judges confidently. Know what is in your notebook and make some notes on index cards to remind you of important points.

Practice: Before the science fair begins, prepare a list of several questions you think you might be asked. Think about the answers and about how your display can help to support them. Have a friend or parent ask you questions and answer them out loud. Knowing your work thoroughly helps you feel more confident when you're asked about it.

Appearance: Dress and act in a way that shows you take your project seriously. Visitors and judges should get the impression that you're interested in the project and that you take pride in answering their questions about it.

Remember: Don't block your exhibit. Stand to the side when someone is looking at it.

Projects about chemistry have special needs with respect to displays. You cannot show the chemical changes as they take place. Instead, photograph or draw them. Many chemical changes are colorful, so use color to make pictures more striking. Show the materials used at the start of the reaction and those produced at the end of the reaction by enclosing them in containers such as sealed petri dishes or plastic bags that you mount on a display. Photograph or draw any special laboratory tools and the laboratory apparatus you set up. Be inventive about different ways of showing what took place.

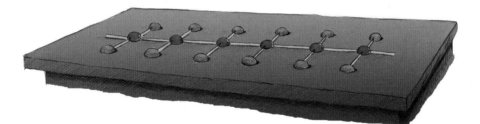

Safety First

Experimenting with chemicals can be dangerous unless certain precautions are taken. Although the experiments in this book mostly use everyday household chemicals, it's your responsibility to use them only as directed. The precautions necessary to prevent accidents and to make the experiments safe and enjoyable are easy to follow.

✔ Never taste any materials listed in this book unless specifically directed to do so. Never put your fingers to your mouth while working on an experiment.

✔ Always wash your hands with warm water and soap after an experiment. Also, wash the surfaces on which you have carried out the experiment.

✔ Never use a mercury thermometer because exposure to mercury is dangerous; use mercury-free alternatives, such as thermometers containing alcohol.

✔ Wear goggles (safety glasses) in experiments as directed. All chemists wear goggles when working in the laboratory. Goggles can be purchased in hardware or dollar stores.

✔ Be sure to have **an adult** supervise your work or do part of it as the directions require.

✔ When using certain solvents, adequate ventilation is necessary, such as an exhaust fan or an open window.

✔ Some solvents are flammable and should not be used near a flame.

✔ Wear plastic gloves when handling chemicals. The thin disposable gloves that may be used on either hand and are sold in packs of about one hundred in dollar stores or hardware stores are very convenient for this purpose.

✔ Some chemicals should not be flushed down the sink or thrown into the garbage. Instructions will be given for disposal of any such materials used in an experiment.

✔ Consideration must always be given to safety when working with chemicals. Therefore, it's essential that **all investigations and science fair projects be approved by a responsible adult.** Where warranted, the experimentation should take place **under adult supervision.** If there are any questions about safety, **the adult** should be sure to obtain the approval of a science teacher before allowing the experiments.

✔ It's a good idea to wear an apron and to work on surfaces that can resist water damage. Covering a surface with newspapers or plastic sheeting will help to protect it.

✔ You should use purified water for experiments unless otherwise stated. Distilled or deionized water sold at the supermarket may be used for this purpose. Natural water from a spring or other source may be safe to drink but isn't considered pure because it contains dissolved solids.

And now, on to the experiments!

CHAPTER 1

Plastics and Polymers Are All Around Us

It was not until after World War II (1939–1945) that the plastics industry started to become important. That was when the name *plastic* first appeared. The name comes from a Greek word meaning "able to be molded." Today, the production of plastics is the fourth largest manufacturing industry in the world. Millions of dollars are spent every year in research laboratories to develop new polymers for old uses and new polymers for uses never dreamed of before.

◄ From sporting goods used for fun, to medical equipment that saves lives, plastics are everywhere.

EXPERIMENT 1.1

Making a Polymer

Question:

What causes fast-drying glue and oil-based paint to form into plastic films (polymers)?

Hypothesis:

When fast-drying glue comes in contact with moisture, or oil-based paint is exposed to the air, the monomers in each polymerize and form a plastic film.

Materials:

- safety goggles
- 2 clean glass micro-scope slides or 2 flat dishes
- tube of extra-fast-drying glue (such as Krazy Glue)
- oil-based house paint or tube of artist's oil paint
- 2 wooden craft or popsicle sticks
- paper and pencil

Did you ever make a polymer? You probably have—although you may not have recognized that you were doing it. Most industrial polymerizations are too hazardous to carry out at home. In this experiment, you will carry out two polymerizations that are safe for you to do. In fact, you may have already done them. This time, you will take a close look at what happens.

The polymers you'll make in this experiment will be formed into plastic films. A film is a thin, flexible sheet like plastic wrap or photographic film. As discussed earlier, polymers are made of repeating parts. The reason that the parts repeat is that the polymers are made by combining small molecules end to end. Added all together, they make up the long polymer chain.

The chains may be linked to each other to form a network polymer. The small molecules that form the polymer are called monomers. If a long polymer is compared to a chain of paper clips, then each monomer is a single paper clip.

In the first part of this experiment, the monomer that you use will be an extra-fast-drying glue.

Procedure:

1. Obtain two clean glass microscope slides or two dishes with flat centers. These will act as supports upon which you will form small pieces of plastic film.

2. Obtain a tube of the extra-fast-drying glue and read the directions for using it. **Safety:** *Find out what to do if you get any on your skin.*

3. Put on your safety goggles.

Figure 3.

A film is formed from an extra-fast-drying glue by spreading several drops of the glue onto a glass slide or flat dish. A popsicle stick is used, if needed, to shape the glue into a circle.

4. Open the tube and allow several drops to fall onto the glass slide or dish. With a wooden stick, quickly spread the glue into a thin layer, as shown in Figure 3. Remove the stick before it gets glued to the dish.

5. Close glue container. Set the slide or dish aside and let the glue harden.

6. Use the stick to check the glue after five minutes to see if it has hardened. If not, check it every five minutes and note how long it takes to become hard. Then discard the stick into a waste container. You may take off the safety goggles.

7. Slide your fingernail under the edge of the film and carefully peel it off the slide or dish. What does the film feel like? How do you think it is able to act as a glue? You should have a rather soft, flexible, transparent film.

Once the film has formed, it can no longer act as a glue. The gluing takes place while the liquid is still polymerizing. At that stage, the liquid penetrates the surfaces around it. The film that forms glues the surfaces together.

Place the film onto a sheet of paper and label it. Store it away for a later experiment. Next, you will make a polymer from oil paint.

1. Apply a layer of any oil-based house paint or artist's oil paint to the second glass slide or dish.

2. Set it aside to harden.

3. Check the paint layer for hardness with a clean wooden stick once every hour. Find out how long it takes the paint to fully harden.

4. When fully hardened, carefully peel off the film as before.

5. How does this film feel? How does it compare to the other one?

   The paint film may feel a little harder than the glue film. It becomes harder the longer it stands. Label and store this film for use in a later experiment.

Results and Conclusions

Neither film actually forms by drying. Although there may be solvents that evaporate in the fast-drying glue and in the oil paint, this evaporation does not cause the glue or oil to become a film. What happens is that each polymerizes.

Oil paint contains monomers that connect to each other to form polymers in the presence of the oxygen in the air. Commercial paints contain compounds to speed up this process. The paint films are the polymerized oils. That explains why you should always store unused paint with the lid on tight.

Fast-drying glue polymerizes almost immediately. It is made up almost entirely of a very reactive monomer (either methyl-2-cyanoacrylate or ethyl-2-cyanoacrylate). When the monomer encounters moisture or certain impurities, it undergoes almost instant polymerization.

Most surfaces, including the plate or slide used in this experiment, have a little moisture from the air or a bit of impurity on them. That is

Science Project Ideas

- Auto body filler is made by a polymerization reaction that takes place fairly rapidly. A tiny amount of hardener (scientists call this the initiator) is added to the monomer. Then it is pressed into the space and shaped. Find out what the monomer is and show the reaction that takes place to form the polymer. Identify the initiator. Prepare a clay mold of a simple object, such as a coin, by first pressing clay around the coin and then carefully removing the clay. **With an adult,** bring the mold to an auto-body repair station. Explain your chemistry project about polymers and that you want to prepare a molded article using auto-body filler. Ask the shop operator to fill the clay mold for you. Be sure that none of the clay overlaps the filler because you need to be able to remove the mold when it is hard. Usually, the repair people are willing to help a student with a project. Observe the safety precautions that the operator takes while preparing the filler and using it.

enough to cause the immediate polymerization. Note that acrylic paints don't polymerize when painted onto a surface because they are already polymers. An acrylic paint mixture is made up of tiny globs of polymer in water. Once the paint is brushed on a surface, the water starts to evaporate. As the water evaporates, the globs move closer to each other and soon join together to form a film. They join each other just the way oil globules floating on water or fat globules in soup join when pushed together by a spoon.

While the filler is hardening, carefully feel its temperature. Any warmth is a sign of a chemical reaction that is taking place. Allow the filler to become very hard. When cool and hard, carefully remove the mold. You have made your own polymerized, molded article. Describe your project in a paper, show the reactions, and exhibit the final product. You can instead make the polymer yourself from an auto-body putty (such as Bondo) that is sold in stores. Be sure to follow the instructions for safe usage.

- Can you set up conditions where an instant glue cannot work? To do this, all impurities and moisture must be removed from the surfaces that you wish to glue together. The surfaces you select to glue should be hard and flat. They should be thoroughly washed and dried and then cleaned with solvents such as kerosene or other water-insoluble solvent. Be careful not to leave lint on the surfaces.

EXPERIMENT 1.2

A Simple Model of a Polymer

Question:

What does a chain of polymer atoms look like?

Hypothesis:

A simple model of a short polymer chain segment can show the structure of a polymer and how atoms are bonded into a chain.

Materials:

- small gumdrops (or clay balls or Styrofoam balls), at least 6 of one color and 12 of another color
- box of toothpicks
- tabletop
- paper and pencil

The chains of atoms that make up polymers are often thousands or even millions of atoms long. You can get an idea of what a polymer looks like by constructing a simple model of a short segment of it. Then, you can imagine the polymer by picturing in your mind the segment repeating itself over and over again to make up the long chain. The segment model that you construct will show the atoms and their connections to other atoms. What the model won't show you is what an atom or molecule or polymer really looks like. In fact, you will make your model out of gumdrops and toothpicks.

The long chains of many polymers are built of linked carbon atoms. The carbon atoms form a backbone to which other atoms or groups of atoms are attached. You will start by constructing a segment of the carbon backbone of such a polymer. You will use small gumdrops all of the same color to represent carbon atoms. Instead of gumdrops, you may use any other soft candy that can be rounded, or you can make clay balls or use Styrofoam balls. Toothpicks will represent the chemical bonds that tie each atom to the next one. If the gumdrops are a little stale, that helps prevent sticky fingers.

The model you will be making in this experiment matches the way many chemistry books show diagrams of polymer structures. The diagrams show all the atoms as if they were on a flat surface like a table. This will give you a two-dimensional (planar) model. In reality, polymer structures are three-dimensional; they extend above and below as well as on the flat surface. We will get to that later.

Figure 4.

(a)

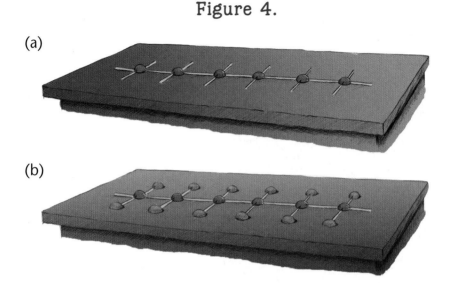

(b)

a) This is a model of the carbon backbone of a six-carbon segment of a polymer chain. The gumdrops represent carbon atoms, and the toothpicks are chemical bonds.

b) This is a hydrocarbon model of a six-carbon segment of a polymer chain. Two hydrogen atoms represented by darkened gumdrops are bonded to each carbon atom. The two end toothpicks are extended to be attached to another segment at each end. The model represents the simplest hydrocarbon polymer.

Procedure:

1. Put one bond (toothpick) partway into a carbon atom (gumdrop). Insert the other end of the toothpick bond partway into another carbon atom (another gumdrop of the same color).

2. Use a second toothpick to bond one of the two carbon atoms to a third one. Continue until you have made a chain that is six carbon atoms long. A carbon atom is stable when it forms four bonds to atoms.

3. Insert additional toothpicks into each gumdrop until all have four bonds to which other atoms can be attached. Remember to keep all the atoms resting on the table top. Make sure the free end of each toothpick is as far as possible from the other toothpick ends.

How many toothpicks did you use? How many bonds does your model have? See Figure 4a.

Your model should have nineteen toothpicks representing nineteen bonds. Of these, five bonds are used to connect the six carbon atoms to each other in a line. The other fourteen bonds each have one free end that is available to link to other atoms. So far, you have formed a segment with a six-carbon backbone.

The simplest atom that can be connected to the carbon atoms is hydrogen. Molecules that contain only carbon and hydrogen are called hydrocarbons. Let's see what the simplest hydrocarbon polymer looks like.

4. To represent hydrogen atoms, use gumdrops of a different color from that used for carbon atoms. Place one hydrogen atom (gumdrop of different color) onto the free end of one of the bonds on each carbon atom.

5. Repeat for a second bond. The two end carbon atoms will each have one bond left with a free end. Leave these empty. How many hydrogen atoms did you attach to your six-carbon backbone?

Results and Conclusions

Your model (see Figure 4b) now represents a segment of a hydrocarbon polymer. It should show a backbone of six carbon atoms with two hydrogen atoms connected to each. There should be a total of twelve hydrogen atoms. The two end carbon atoms should each have one bond with a free end. They represent the links to the next segments of the polymer chain.

Chemistry books often use what is called a structural formula in order to show the arrangement of atoms in a polymer. A structural formula looks very much like your model except that chemical symbols instead of gumdrops are used for the atoms and a single line is used for the bond. Figure 5 shows the structural formula of the six-carbon segment you have constructed.

Figure 5.

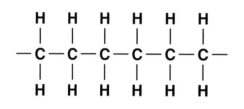

In this structural formula of a six-carbon segment of a polymer chain, each atom is identified by its symbol. Each bond holding two atoms together is shown by a straight line.

Imagine how your model would look with another such hydrocarbon segment attached to each end of your polymer segment. Next, imagine additional segments attached to each end, on and on, until your chain has several thousand carbon atoms. You now have a mental picture of the simplest hydrocarbon polymer chain. The name of this hydrocarbon polymer is polyethylene. Polyethylene is used to make food wraps, stiff or flexible plastic containers, telephone and power cables, toys, and trash bags.

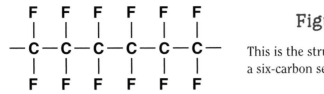

Figure 6.

This is the structural formula of a six-carbon segment of Teflon.

Hydrogen atoms are not the only atoms that can be attached to carbon atoms. Chlorine atoms, oxygen atoms, nitrogen atoms, carbon atoms, and many others can be substituted for the hydrogen atoms.

Many of the substituted atoms can have various atoms attached to them in more than one kind of arrangement. Furthermore, there are polymers that don't have a carbon backbone. Silly Putty, for instance, has a silicon backbone. All these combinations make a tremendous variety of polymers possible.

On a piece of paper, write the structural formula of a segment of a polymer with a six-carbon backbone and with all the hydrogen atoms replaced by fluorine atoms. This structural formula is shown in Figure 6. Its common name is Teflon. Teflon is a polymer that is commonly used as a nonstick surface of cookware.

EXPERIMENT 1.3

Arrangement of Carbon Bonds in Space

Question:

How can you arrange four atoms bonded to a carbon atom to be farthest apart from each other?

Hypothesis:

Since nature is three-dimensional, not flat, bonded atoms can extend in any direction. A tetrahedron shape will allow the four atoms to be as far apart as possible.

Materials:

- small gumdrops, at least 6 of one color and 12 of another color
- box of toothpicks
- Styrofoam board, at least 25 cm x 15 cm (10 in x 6 in)

The instructions for making the model in Experiment 1.2 stated that the free ends of the bonds (toothpicks) should be set as far apart as possible. Because you laid out a two-dimensional (flat) model, the farthest apart the four bonds could be was when they pointed at the four corners of a square. However, atoms and molecules actually exist in three-dimensional space.

When atoms that are bonded to a central carbon atom can spread out in any direction, there is another possible arrangement that allows the bonds to get even farther apart from each other. Bonds coming from the carbon atom would have this arrangement if they were pointing to the four corners of a tetrahedron. Figure 7 shows this arrangement.

This experiment will look at a model constructed with the tetrahedral arrangement, the one found in nature rather than in the pages of a book.

Procedure:

To construct a model of a carbon backbone with bonds in the tetra-hedral arrangement around each carbon atom, start as before with toothpicks and gumdrops.

1. Place four toothpicks into one carbon atom, inserting the toothpicks as far from each other as you can. Keep Figure 7 in mind. Turn your carbon atom in various directions to check that the bonds are spaced as far from each other as they can get. If you spaced the four bonds of the carbon atom perfectly, each would form an angle of 109.5 degrees with any of the other bonds. An approximation will do for this experiment.

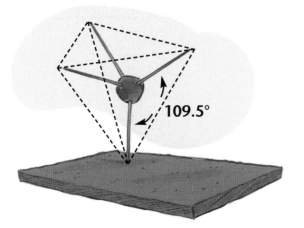

Figure 7.

The tetrahedral arrangement of single bonds around a central carbon atom is shown. The dotted lines show the tetrahedral shape. Each bond is at an angle of 109.5 degrees to the others.

2. Hold your carbon atom by one toothpick and insert that toothpick vertically into a Styrofoam board. Make up another carbon atom with toothpicks spaced in the tetrahedral arrangement. Stick that one into the board.

3. Make four more such carbons atoms, each with its four tetrahedral bonds (toothpicks).

   The carbon atoms are now ready to be assembled into one segment.

4. Remove one of the bonds from one carbon atom.

5. Attach a second carbon atom by one of its bonds to the first atom by replacing the bond that was removed. You now have a two-carbon segment.

6. In the same way, attach to the chain each of the other four carbon atoms that you have prepared. Each time, one of the bonds replaces the one that is removed.

Results and Conclusions

Do the carbon atoms lie in a straight line? Figure 8 shows a model that was constructed using the above instructions. In this model, the six-carbon atoms don't lie in a straight line. Rather, they have a jagged arrangement due to the tetrahedral arrangement of bonds.

Save your model for Experiment 1.5.

The arrangement of your model depends in part on how each carbon atom was turned when joined to the next one. In fact, there are other possible arrangements besides the one in Figure 8. Different strands of the same polymer may have different shapes.

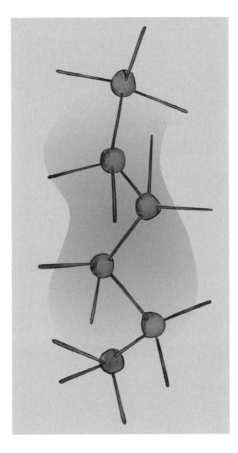

Figure 8.

A toothpick/gumdrop model of the six-carbon backbone segment of a polymer chain shows the tetrahedral arrangement of bonds around each carbon atom.

Science Project Idea

- If you have a four-carbon backbone of a chain, there are two different ways that carbon atoms can be connected. The four atoms can be attached one to the next, or three carbon atoms can be attached to one central atom. Construct permanent tetrahedral models that can be displayed to show both arrangements. Include the bonded hydrogen atoms. How does this add variety to the polymeric hydrocarbons that can be produced?

EXPERIMENT 1.4

Making Slime: Cross-Linking

Question:

Can separate chains of polymer molecules link together and form a solid?

Hypothesis:

The polymer in glue can cross–link and make polymer chains. The resulting slimy substance can be kneaded into a plastic ball.

Materials:

- safety goggles
- small glass jar
- paper cup
- borax (20 Mule Team Borax or other brand)
- plastic gloves (thin, loose-fitting, discard-able after one use)
- Elmer's Glue-All or White Glue
- water
- measuring spoons
- wooden craft or popsicle sticks
- coin
- page from a newspaper
- thin plastic wrap
- pen with washable ink
- refrigerator
- plastic garbage bag and tie
- table

In this experiment, you will carry out a chemical reaction. In a chemical reaction, substances are changed into different substances by reorganizing which atoms are connected.

The reaction in this experiment will cause a link (chemical bond) to form between one polymer chain and another one near it. You will start with long chains separate from each other and finish with chains that are linked together. One chain may become connected to one, two, three, or even more other chains, depending on how the reaction is carried out. In fact, multiple links between chains can form all over the solution. This process is called cross-linking (see Figure 9).

The product of this particular experiment will be a partly cross-linked polymer. The product will be very much like Slime or Silly Putty. The polymer that will be cross-linked is called polyvinyl acetate. It is the glue ingredient in Elmer's Glue-All or Elmer's White Glue. Borax will form the bridges (cross-links) between one chain and the next.

Figure 9.

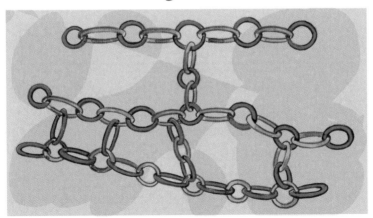

Each link in the diagram represents a group of atoms in a segment of cross-linked polymer chains. The cross-links may be made up of the same links or of links made of a different atom or group of atoms.

Procedure:

Safety: *Handle the dry borax with a spoon, not your fingers. Wear plastic gloves since some people are allergic to dry borax. Be careful not to inhale the dry borax. Wash your hands after handling any chemicals and after the experiment is finished. Do not allow small children to play with your product since they may try to put it their mouths. Do not put the product that you make on top of any fabric such as a cloth or your clothing; you may not get it out.*

1. Put on your safety goggles and plastic gloves.

2. Mix together 1 tablespoon of white glue and 1 tablespoon of water in a small glass jar.

3. In a paper cup, place about ⅛ teaspoon of borax into 1 tablespoon of water. Stir with a wooden stick until all the borax is dissolved.

4. While stirring the glue mixture in the jar, add the borax solution to it. A slime will form, leaving a little water behind in the jar. Pour this water back into the paper cup.

5. Pour a little water over your slime to cleanse it and add that water to the paper cup.

6. Now you can play with your slime. Remove your gloves and knead the slime with your hands. When you break the slime in half, can it be kneaded back into a whole? Shape it into a ball. Does the ball bounce? What happens when you press the ball downward gently? What happens when you place the ball on a table and give it a hard slap? Press a coin into the slime. Does it hold the shape of the coin? What happens when you tear or cut the slime? Can it lift print from a newspaper? Draw on a thin film of plastic with washable ink. Can

you get your slime to lift off the ink? Compare how the slime behaves when pulled apart slowly and carefully and when pulled apart rapidly. What happens to it if you stick a piece on the outside wall of the refrigerator?

7. When you have completed the experiment, place the wooden stick and the paper cup with the water in it into a sealed plastic bag and discard the bag in the garbage. Don't discard any of it down the drain because there may still be some glue in it. You can store your slime in a sealed plastic bag. Keep it in the refrigerator to prevent mold. Should you have to discard the slime, throw it in the garbage can, not down the drain. You may remove the safety goggles.

Results and Conclusions

At the start, the glue has in it millions of extremely long chains of the polymer, polyvinyl acetate. The addition of borax causes links to form between the chains. Many of the chains become tied together by one or more links. The amount of cross-linking depends on the proportions of the reactants. A little more of the borax will make the product almost solid, while less of the borax will make the product more like a gel.

The slime can be stretched slowly but will break with sharp edges when pulled rapidly. A ball of slime bounces when dropped. Your slime was probably depressed by the coin, although the coin's imprint didn't show. The slime doesn't lift off the print from newspaper (commercial Slime lifts colored print), but it does remove the color of the washable ink from the plastic. The separated parts can be kneaded together. When placed on the side of the refrigerator, the slime stays there.

The more cross-linking there is, the stiffer and more solid the product becomes. If all the chains were to be linked together in many places, the product would be a solid. Chemists are usually able to vary the quantities of ingredients to control the amount of cross-linking that takes place.

Now that you have observed some of the properties of the slime you made, you can investigate how changes in the recipe affect the properties. Vary the proportions of the glue, water, and borax to observe the differences. Make a chart of the proportions, your hypotheses as to what will happen, and the actual results.

Slime, Silly Putty, Gak, Ooze, and other such products are called non-Newtonian liquids because they don't flow the way ordinary liquids do. The differences that you saw are due to the entangling of chains and the cross-links that pull the chains back in place when they start to flow a little. As you can see, the long length of the polymer chains causes them to have certain properties different from that of ordinary molecules.

💡 Science Project Ideas

- Compare the properties of commercial Slime and Silly Putty to the slime that you made. How do they behave when stretched slowly or quickly? Do they bounce? How well? When placed on a vertical surface, do they flow? How long does a dent made in them last? Do they pick up ink from a surface? Do they have other properties that your slime did not have? The Slime sold in stores is made with guar gum and borax. Silly Putty is prepared from borax and silicone oil. Other such products are made with polyvinyl alcohol and borax.

- Many other slime-type materials can be made. What is the effect of separately adding each of the following to the mixture you used in Experiment 1.4: a few drops of glycerin, some talcum powder, some ground-up chalk (you may have to adjust the basic ingredients by adding more water)? Try some other additives to see their effect.

- Look for products containing polymers that might form cross-links with borax. These include water-soluble polymers that have alcohol or acetate groups on them. Polyvinyl alcohol (PVA) is known to cross-link with borax. Try searching the supermarket and drugstore shelves for water-containing products such as hair styling gels that list PVA or a copolymer of PVA as an ingredient. Test the products to see if there is evidence of cross-linking when combined with a borax solution. Thickening or stiffening is evidence of cross-linking. Note that ingredients on labels are listed in order of their weight—in order for the experiment to work, PVA needs to be one of the first products listed. Also, look for food products that use natural gums (such as guar gums) as thickeners in water. Test these products to see if they are cross-linked by borax.

EXPERIMENT 1.5

A Model Problem

Question:

How can you calculate the length of a model of a polyethylene strand that is a thousand atoms long?

Hypothesis:

Every segment in the strand has the same distance between the atoms. You can multiply that distance by the number of atoms, minus one, to calculate the strand's length.

Materials:

- model of a polymer segment from Experiment 1.3
- centimeter ruler

In Experiment 1.3, you constructed a six-carbon segment of a polymer called polyethylene. Suppose you wanted to make a model of a polyethylene strand with a backbone of 1,000 atoms. How long would this model be?

Procedure:

1. Measure the distance between the centers of two carbon atoms in the model that you constructed in Experiment 1.3.

2. Use this measurement to calculate the length of a model that is 1,000 atoms long.

   Here is one solution to the above problem. Let us say that the measured distance between the centers of the two carbon atoms in the model is 5.0 cm. There are 999 bonds between 1,000 atoms. To simplify calculations, we'll say that there are 1,000 bonds. The length of the polymer model from carbon atom to carbon atom will be:

   $$1{,}000 \text{ atoms} \times \frac{5.0 \text{ cm}}{\text{atom}} = 5{,}000 \text{ cm or } 50 \text{ m (over 50 yards)}$$

Results and Conclusions

This model has a problem! It is too long. However, there is an easy way to deal with this problem. It isn't really necessary to build the entire polymer chain to make a model of polyethylene. Only one or a few of the repeating segments will do the job. In fact, the model you've already constructed is good enough since the same segment is repeated over and over again in the long chains.

Figure 5 showed the structural formula of the six-carbon polyethylene segment you constructed in Experiment 1.3. An abbreviated shortened structural formula of polyethylene is usually written as shown in

Figure 10.

(a) 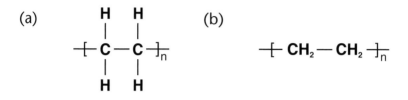 (b)

a) Structural formula of polyethylene.
b) Abbreviated form of the structural formula of polyethylene.

Figure 10a and can be further abbreviated as shown in Figure 10b. A two-carbon segment is usually shown instead of a one-carbon segment because polyethylene is made from ethylene, a molecule containing two carbon atoms. The bracket shows the repeating unit and the dash through the bracket represents the bond to the next segment. The "n" stands for the number of repeating segments. Since the number is usually not known, an "x" is often substituted for the "n."

See Appendix A for uses of some hydrocarbon polymers.

As pointed out earlier, the hydrogen atoms on a polymeric carbon chain may be replaced by many other atoms or groups. Each of these replacements changes the characteristics of the polymer and adds to the possible uses. Even the arrangement of the replacement groups, whether all on one side of the chain or staggered or random, affects the properties of polymers. Variations such as these make it possible to produce over sixty thousand different polymers each year.

Science Project Ideas

- Construct a two-carbon model of a polymer segment that has one chlorine atom substituted for each hydrogen atom. Draw the corresponding structural formula.

- Make a series of drawings (or a series of models) of different configurations of a three-carbon segment of a hydrocarbon polymer chain. All three carbon atoms may rotate separately around its bond to the next carbon atom.

- Show with a series of drawings how the arrangement of carbon atoms in the carbon backbone of several adjacent polymer chains can cause the chains to become entangled.

- Draw the structural formulas of a six-carbon segment of a polymer where two of the hydrogen atoms have been replaced by chlorine. How many different such polymers can be constructed? Explain.

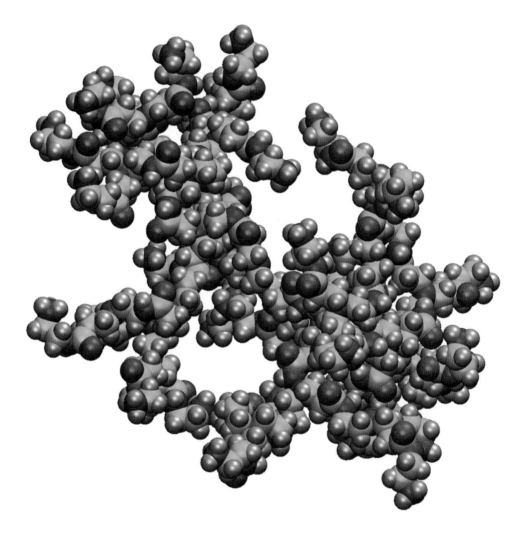

CHAPTER 2

Some Properties of Polymers

Although we can never see inside molecules or atoms with our eyes, scientists have developed all kinds of tools to help us find out what is there. These bits of information are something like the information obtained when six blind men examined an elephant, as told in a fable in India many years ago.

The first blind man approached the elephant and fell against it. He decided that an elephant is like a wall.

The second blind man felt the tusk and concluded that an elephant is like a spear.

The third grasped the trunk and thought that an elephant is like a snake.

◄ Technicians study models of polymer molecules, such as this one, to develop medical equipment.

The fourth felt the elephant's knee and said that an elephant is like a tree.

The fifth touched the elephant's ear and thought it obvious that an elephant is like a fan.

The sixth grabbed the elephant's swinging tail and concluded that an elephant is like a rope.

The six blind men debated loudly, each sure that only he was right. They never found out what an elephant is really like.

Like the six blind men, chemists also find out little bits and pieces in their experiments, but there is a big difference in how the chemists share this information. Chemists are part of an international community of scientists who present their newly gained knowledge as quickly as possible via meetings, publications in journals, and on the Internet. Based on the collected information, chemists have been able to build up, bit by bit, detailed pictures of the parts of matter, pictures of what is too small to ever see. They know what the "elephant" is like. They are able to see inside of matter in ways that would have been considered magical before our time. And chemists have used this knowledge to build materials that have never existed before on Earth, or even perhaps, in the entire universe.

In this chapter, the experiments will examine some polymers and how their properties are related to their extreme length.

EXPERIMENT 2.1

Polymers That Melt

Question:
Is a glue stick a thermoset or a thermoplastic?

Hypothesis:
Since glue sticks can be remelted, they are thermoplastic.

Materials:
- **an adult**
- safety goggles
- glue stick that melts at low temperature or glue gun with glue stick
- stove with burners
- pot of water
- sink
- metal tongs
- metal pot lid

Some solid polymers melt when heated. Polymers that can melt are called thermoplastic. When melted, thermoplastic polymers can be poured into molds where they harden to form the desired products. Thermoplastic polymers can also be extruded (pushed through a narrow opening) to form fibers (threads that can be thin or thick). In addition, the solidified products can be remelted.

Other solid polymers are called thermosets. They don't melt at all when heated. Instead, they end up scorched or even burned. As a result, thermosets can only be molded into a desired shape as they are formed.

The following experiment illustrates one of these two types of solid polymers.

Procedure:

1. In a craft store, look through the assortment of glue sticks available. Find one whose label says that it melts below the temperature of boiling water. See later instructions if you can only find glue sticks for glue guns.

2. Put your safety goggles on.

3. **Under the supervision of an adult**, boil a pan of water.

4. Use tongs to hold the glue stick at its top. Lower the glue stick halfway into the boiling water. Does the glue stick melt?

5. Raise it and, with the tongs, quickly press the hot stick onto a metal pot cover. Does the stick spread out a bit?

6. Put the end of the glue stick back in the water as before. Does it melt again?

   If you cannot obtain a glue stick that melts at low temperature, **have an adult** use a glue gun to melt a glue stick. Allow some of the melt to drip onto a solid metal surface such as the pot lid (see Figure 11). Then, **the adult** should touch the solidified melt with the hot tip of the glue gun. Does the solid melt again?

7. Pour the water into the sink. The plastic can be wedged off the metal and thrown into the garbage.

   Was the glue stick thermoplastic or thermosetting?

Figure 11.

The hot end of the glue stick is lowered into boiling water and then pressed onto the top of a pot cover.

push gently

Results and Conclusions

Thermosets can't melt to a liquid because they are made of chains with enough cross-links between them so that the chains can't slip past each other. In the liquid state, particles are able to move around each other. Since extensively cross-linked polymer chains can't move past each other, they can't be melted and will burn if the temperature gets high enough.

Thermoplastic polymers can be compared to water that is frozen into a block of ice and is then melted to liquid water again. The process can be repeated again and again. Thermosetting polymers are more like the

Table 1.

Properties of Thermosets Compared to Thermoplastic Polymers

Type of Solid Polymer	What Happens When Heated	How They Are Shaped	Percent of Total Plastics Used Today
Thermoplastic	Melts	By molding or extruding	85
Thermosetting	Scorches and eventually burns	As formed	15

white of an egg. If you boil an egg for ten minutes and then examine the white, you will find that it is a white solid. There is no way that you can return it back to the liquid egg white. If you keep increasing the heat, the egg white will burn.

All solid polymers are either thermoplastic, which melts, or thermosetting, which burns. The glue stick melted when heated, so it was thermoplastic.

Which type of solid polymer do you think is likely to be produced the most? See Table 1 for the answer.

EXPERIMENT 2.2

Making and Shaping Thermosetting Plastic

Question:

Can you make a thermosetting plastic using epoxy putty? Can you test its properties with heat?

Hypothesis:

Kneaded epoxy putty will harden. If it burns under heat rather than melts, then it has gone through the cross-linking process and is a thermosetting plastic.

Materials:

- **an adult**
- safety goggles
- disposable plastic gloves
- epoxy putty (can be obtained in hardware stores)
- plastic knife
- candle and matches
- tongs

The following experiment will enable you to make a thermosetting plastic and then to test its thermosetting properties.

Procedure:

1. Put on safety goggles and a pair of disposable plastic gloves. Obtain a roll of plumber's epoxy putty.

2. With a plastic knife, gently cut two slices about 1 cm (⅓ in) from the end of the roll. You can probably see the different colors of the two ingredients.

3. Gently put one of the slices aside. Knead and twist the other slice until it is all one color. As you knead it, do you feel any temperature change? A temperature change indicates that a chemical reaction may have taken place.

4. Feel the unkneaded putty to find out if its temperature has also changed.

Figure 12.

After you have shaped the kneaded putty into a disk, punch in two eyes, a nose, and a mouth.

5. Shape the kneaded putty, now all one color, into a disk. Punch in two eyes, a nose, and a mouth (see Figure 12).

6. Place it on a countertop. After one minute, feel its temperature. Feel the temperature of the unkneaded putty, too. Were there any changes?

7. Discard the plastic gloves and remove the goggles. Let the two pieces of putty stand for about twenty minutes without touching them. Then, note any changes.

8. Being careful not to press or squeeze the unkneaded putty, leave both pieces until the next day in a cool, safe place where no one will touch them.

9. The next day, compare both pieces. Gently press each piece to check hardness. Use tongs to pick up the small piece of putty that you kneaded and shaped.

10. Carry out the next step outdoors or under an exhaust fan that vents to the outside. **Ask an adult** to light a candle.

11. With tongs, hold the small piece of shaped putty in the flame. Does it melt? Does it burn? After cooling, it may be safely discarded in the trash.

Results and Conclusions

When epoxy putty is kneaded, a heat-producing reaction takes place. The two parts of the putty combine with each other to form a polymer. Is a thermosetting or thermoplastic polymer formed? Did cross-linking occur? How do you know? What happened to the unkneaded putty? Did it change in any way?

You can expect to find no change in the unkneaded putty. When the two parts required to make the polymer are not intermixed, no polymerization can occur.

Safety: *It isn't safe to test this piece to see if it melts or burns. You need to get rid of it. To do this safely, knead this piece as you did the other, taking the same precautions as before. Let it harden and then discard it.*

💡 Science Project Ideas

In any experiment that uses heat, be sure to wear your safety goggles and to do your work **with adult supervision.** Handle hot solids with tongs.

- Is the product of an instant glue a thermosetting or a thermoplastic polymer? **Under adult supervision,** investigate using the polymer film that you made in Experiment 1.3. You can also test the dried oil paint and the slime that you made in Experiment 1.4. Explain the results.

- Make a film out of Elmer's Glue-all or Elmer's White Glue. **Under adult supervision,** find out if it is a thermosetting or a thermoplastic polymer. How does it compare to the slime that you made from the glue?

- Obtain a glue stick that melts below the boiling point of water. Repeatedly melt a piece of it and allow it to harden again. What changes, if any, do you observe in the plastic?

EXPERIMENT 2.3

Some Polymers Like Water

Question:

How do disposable baby diapers retain moisture?

Hypothesis:

Disposable diapers must contain a polymer that absorbs water.

Materials:

- safety goggles
- 1 medium-sized disposable baby diaper
- scissors
- white sheet of paper
- stapler
- measuring cup
- tap water
- colorless, wide-mouth, quart-sized glass jar
- glass-marking pen
- small cup
- teaspoon
- table salt
- sink

Most polymers are insoluble in water, meaning they don't dissolve in water. So if you add a teaspoonful of an insoluble polymer to water and stir it up, the polymer will remain unchanged in the water. This is unlike salt, which is quite soluble in water and will disappear (dissolve) into water upon stirring.

There are a few polymer solids that water can penetrate. Such polymers may swell in water, form gels, or even dissolve. These polymers are hydrophilic (from the Greek words *hydro* meaning "water" and *philos* for "dear" or "loving"). Hydrophilic polymers "like" water.

When polymers like water, they can be used to absorb water. Such polymers may be found in diapers and sometimes in packets enclosed in packages of fresh meat to help absorb fluids. How effective is the polymer in a diaper in absorbing water?

This experiment involves several procedures and results.

Procedure:

1. Put on safety goggles. The moisture-absorbing material to be used in this experiment, sodium polyacrylate, isn't toxic. However, always protect your eyes when working with commercial chemicals. Don't discard any materials from this experiment until you are instructed to do so.

2. Cut away and discard all but the long, cotton-like padded section in the center of a baby diaper. Be sure to leave some plastic intact along the edges of this padded section, which will be called the diaper pad.

3. With scissors, cut across the diaper pad from one side to the other. Make another cut 13 cm (5 in) above the first to make a square piece of diaper pad open at each end.

4. Hold this square over a sheet of white paper and pluck away about 3 cm (1 in) of the cotton-like stuffing from each of the two open ends. Place the removed stuffing on the sheet of paper.

5. Fold the empty part of each end of the diaper pad at least once to cover the open ends. Leave plenty of room for the contents of the diaper pad to expand.

6. Staple the ends closed to seal the diaper pad.

7. Obtain a colorless, wide-mouth, quart-sized glass jar. Use a measuring cup to fill the jar halfway with tap water, keeping a record of how much water you used.

8. With a glass-marking pen, mark the jar on the outside to show the level of the water in the jar.

9. Place the diaper pad into the jar and push it completely under the water. Allow the jar with the pad and water to stand at least twenty minutes. What do you observe? Is the immersed diaper pad swollen with water?

10. Pull the pad out of the water. Allow any drops of water from it to fall back into the jar. Place the wet pad on the table and press it gently with the palm of your hand to see if you can squeeze out any more water. Don't press with your fingers since that may tear through the covering. Can you squeeze any more water out?

11. How much water was used to swell the pad? To find out, you can subtract the quantity of water left in the jar from the quantity with which you started. You already know the quantity at the start. To measure the water left in the jar, pour this water into the measuring cup until there is a full cup.

12. Record the amount of water in the cup, then discard the water into the sink.

13. Keeping a record of the total quantity of water, continue pouring a cupful at a time until the water in the jar is gone.

14. Subtract the total amount of water left in the jar from the amount of water with which you started. The difference equals the quantity of water absorbed by the diaper pad.

Results and Conclusions

The chemical that works this magic is a polymer called sodium polyacrylate. Sodium polyacrylate is extremely hydrophilic.

Is the stuffing inside the diaper made of sodium polyacrylate or is the stuffing just a support for sodium polyacrylate? To find out, here's a clue: Go back to the stuffing placed on the sheet of paper. You will see tiny granules on the paper that dropped out of the stuffing.

How can you test the stuffing and the granules to see which is the sodium polyacrylate? You can do so by using water.

Procedure:

1. Shake the stuffing you removed from the pad over the paper. If you don't have a visible layer of polymer granules, pull out some more stuffing from the diaper and shake it over the paper. If any fluff from the stuffing is on the paper, remove it by gently rolling it into a clump with your fingers.

2. Place the collected granules into a cup and add about 1 cm (½ in) of tap water. Allow this to stand for about twenty minutes.

3. While you're waiting, add water to the stuffing and see if you can squeeze the water out again. Have the granules swelled in the cup? Is the water thick?

4. Keep adding small quantities of water to see how much the granules absorb until there is no change. What happened with the rest of the stuffing?

   What are your conclusions?

Results and Conclusions

The ability of sodium polyacrylate to absorb water has to do with positive and negative electrostatic charge. Sodium polyacrylate has oxygen atoms in it that carry some negative charge. The negative charge is balanced by sodium atoms that carry positive charge. The sodium atoms are bonded to the oxygen atoms as shown in Figure 13a. When placed in water, the water molecules are attracted to both positive and negative sites and cluster around them (Figure 13b). The water gets trapped in the spaces left between the convoluted polymer molecules.

Globules of gel are formed. Enough water can penetrate the polymer to swell it up to many times its own size. Here's how to observe this process:

Procedure:

1. Take a teaspoonful of the thick water into which you added the polymer granules.

2. Sprinkle a little table salt over it. What happens?

3. Before discarding the thick water with the polymer granules, add enough salt to it to liquefy all of it. Fill the container completely with water and pour it down the sink with the water running. Allow the water to run for another thirty seconds.

4. Discard all solids into the garbage, including any unused polymer granules.

Figure 13.

(a)

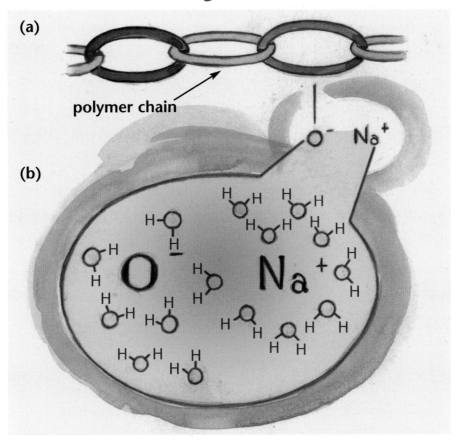

(b)

a) The polymer sodium polyacrylate is represented by a chain in which the links stand for the repeating units. Each link has an oxygen atom (O) bonded to it with a sodium atom (Na) bonded to the oxygen atom. The oxygen and sodium atoms are shown for only one of the segments. The oxygen atom carries some negative charge and the sodium atom carries some positive charge.

b) When sodium polyacrylate is placed in water, it becomes surrounded by water molecules. Hydrogen atoms (H) in the water are attracted to and surround the oxygen atoms in the sodium polyacrylate chain. The oxygen atoms in the water are attracted to the sodium atoms and surround them. These attractions enable water to gradually get between the many chains of polymer. The water will eventually swell the polymer to a large volume. In this drawing, the water molecules have been reduced to show how they face the oxygen and sodium atoms.

Results and Conclusions

Table salt interferes with the ability of the polymer to hold water because table salt has atoms carrying strong negative and positive charge. Salt atoms get between the polymer and the water and interfere with the polymer's ability to hold the water. As a result, some water comes out of the polymer. Other compounds with charged sites in them, such as baking soda and vinegar, have the same effect.

The manufacture of disposable diapers is one of the most important uses of polymers. The water–absorbing material in plastic diapers is in the form of crystals that are held, or supported, by a cotton-like synthetic

 Science Project Ideas

- How does the volume of tap water compare to the volume of purified water absorbed by a diaper pad? For purified water, you can use distilled or deionized water or water from a dehumidifier. Investigate and explain the result.

- Carry out experiments on a diaper pad to find out how its ability to absorb water changes when dissolved sugar is present in tap water. Does the quantity of sugar make a difference? (Sugar does not have charged particles in it.)

- Allow a water-swollen diaper pad to stay on a counter top for several days. Does the swelling decrease? Does the pad continue to feel wet? Explain your observations. Continue your experiment for as long as you can to see if any changes occur.

fiber. Since these crystals turn into a thick gel when they absorb water, we must be careful about discarding them properly. They must not be thrown into toilets because they will block the water flow. Also, these diapers can't be worn by children playing in swimming pools because the gel can leak into the water and plug pool filters and water outlets.

After use, disposable diapers must be put into a garbage container and shipped to a facility that can safely treat them as solid waste. Since 27.4 billion disposable diapers are used every year in the United States, they have a powerful impact on the environment. Disposable diapers result in 3.4 million tons of landfill waste.

- How much of a solution of 0.9 g of table salt dissolved in 99 mL of water is absorbed by a test sample of diaper pad? This is approximately the same concentration as the salts in baby urine. Would you expect a diaper to be more or less absorbent in actual use than when tested with tap water?

- Compare different brands of diapers to see which is the best buy based on the amount of simulated "urine" absorbed. Be sure the diapers are made for the same weight range of a baby.

- How does temperature affect the water absorbency of sodium polyacrylate? Investigate and explain your results. How does this affect the use of a diaper?

- Compare the absorbency of a diaper pad to that of an equal weight of paper towel. Which is preferable to use for a diaper? Why? Which is preferable to clean up a spill of water on the floor? Why?

EXPERIMENT 2.4

Styrofoam: A Polymer That Does Not Like Water

Question:

Some polymers are ideal for cups and packaging because they don't dissolve in water. Can other liquids dissolve them?

Hypothesis:

Styrofoam is polystyrene that has been expanded with air. Acetone will replace the air in expanded polystyrene, causing it to collapse.

Materials:

- small flat square or chunk of non-foamed polystyrene (such as the bottom of a transparent plastic drinking glass, a chunk from pen casing, or casings for hair dryers and other electrical equipment; these items are labeled <6> in the Plastic Resin Identification Code
- used in recycling).
- acetone (or acetone-type nail polish remover)
- safety goggles
- small glass jar with lid
- metal spoon
- Styrofoam cup
- wide-neck glass jar (neck should be wider than the cup base)
- sink with running water

Foods, liquids, items displayed on racks, and fragile objects are very often encased in plastic for protection and/or for visibility. All the plastic used for such packaging must be waterproof to both keep water from getting in and to keep water from getting out. Such plastics are hydrophobic (from the Greek words *hydro* meaning "water" and *phobos* meaning "fear"). They don't "like" water.

Polystyrene is a hydrocarbon, and like all hydrocarbons it is insoluble in water. You probably already have seen how polystyrene is insoluble in water because it is used for drinking cups and other waterproof materials. It would not be convenient if your cup dissolved when water was poured into it.

Styrofoam is a common name for polystyrene that has been "expanded" with gases during its manufacture. The result is an air-filled material that is white, rigid, lightweight, and spongelike. It is used for hot and cold cups, food trays, and all kinds of packaging that need insulation and/or protection from bangs and bumps. Since it is made of polystyrene and air, we know that it isn't soluble in water.

If these plastics are not soluble in water, is there another liquid that can dissolve them? This experiment will investigate acetone for this purpose. Acetone is a small molecule made of carbon atoms, hydrogen atoms, and an oxygen atom. It is very soluble in water. Will acetone dissolve polystyrene?

Acetone may be purchased in hardware stores. It is also the main ingredient of some nail polish removers. When a nail polish remover contains acetone, the acetone is ordinarily diluted by other ingredients. As a result, if you use acetone-type nail polish remover instead of acetone in this experiment, the changes will take longer to complete and will be less striking. Separate instructions using an acetone-type nail polish remover may be found at the end of this experiment.

Safety: *Acetone is flammable and should be used only where no flame is near. Because it evaporates readily, use it only in a well-ventilated room or outdoors. Wear safety goggles whenever you work with acetone. Keep any container of acetone tightly covered when not in use. You may wish to wear plastic gloves because acetone dries the skin. A little hand cream will remoisturize your skin.*

This experiment has three procedures:

Procedure:

1. Break off a small chunk of non-foamed polystyrene. Pour some acetone into a small glass jar and add your polystyrene sample to it.

2. Stir well with a metal spoon. Does the polystyrene dissolve? Has the sample changed color?

3. Cover the jar and let it stand with occasional shaking for about a half hour. Does the polymer swell in the acetone?

4. Using a metal spoon, lift the sample out of the acetone. Scratch the sample with your fingernail to see if it has softened.

5. After the test is completed, rinse the polystyrene sample with water and discard it into the recycling bin or waste basket.

6. Pour the used acetone down the drain with the water running. Rinse the jar with water and pour the water down the drain. Keep the water running for at least a half minute.

Did the polystyrene dissolve? Did you detect any change in it?

Next, the test with acetone will be repeated on Styrofoam.

Procedure:

1. Put on your safety goggles. **Safety:** *Take the same safety precautions when using acetone as stated before.* Hold a Styrofoam cup centered over a wide-neck jar (see Figure 14). Pour a little acetone, just enough to cover the bottom, into the cup. What happens? What is in the jar? What does the cup look like now?

2. Use the metal spoon to push the Styrofoam cup into the jar. Keep pushing until all the cup is under the acetone. What does the cup look like at this point?

Figure 14.

Pour acetone into a Styrofoam cup. What happens?

3. With the aid of the spoon, retrieve all the soft solid pieces floating in the acetone.

4. Rinse the solid with running water from the sink. You can now safely handle the solid with your fingers.

5. Roll it into a ball.

6. Discard the acetone down the drain with the water running and allow the water to run for at least half a minute afterward.

7. Put the ball down on the sink counter. Did the acetone dissolve the Styrofoam?

8. You have completed the experiment and may remove the safety goggles.

Results and Conclusions

The polystyrene (not expanded) did not dissolve in acetone, but it may have softened a bit. The color of the polystyrene sample may have whitened. You may have detected slight swelling.

The results with the Styrofoam cup were quite different. When acetone is poured into a Styrofoam cup, it goes right through, leaving plastic hanging around a hole in the cup. It is astonishing how quickly the acetone cuts through the cup. Did the acetone dissolve the Styrofoam cup's polystyrene, however? The answer is no. This polystyrene was collapsed to a lump.

You can allow the polystyrene ball to air-dry and then show it off as your collapsed Styrofoam cup.

Next, using an acetone-type nail polish remover as follows, try to make a Styrofoam cup collapse:

Procedure:

1. Put on your safety goggles. **Safety:** *Obey the precautions that need to be taken when working with acetone.*

2. Place a Styrofoam cup upright into a clean glass jar.

3. Pour acetone-type nail polish remover into the Styrofoam cup about one-fourth of the way up. **Safety:** *Keep the jar and its contents away from any flame and in a well-ventilated location and allow it to stand.*

4. Occasionally push the cup downward so as to keep about one-fourth of it under the nail polish remover. You may need to replenish the polish remover.

5. Continue until the entire cup is under the liquid. Then, remove the remains of the cup and squeeze it dry and into a ball.

6. Discard the used polish remover into the sink drain and run the water down the drain for about a minute.

7. You may remove the safety goggles.

Results and Conclusions

Acetone does not dissolve polystyrene whether or not the polymer is expanded. Styrofoam collapses because acetone replaces the air in it.

You can also make Styrofoam collapse with acetone-type nail polish remover. The speed at which the collapse takes place depends on the proportion of acetone in the polish remover.

Expanded polystyrene has many important uses, such as in insulation, drinking cups, and packaging. However, this foam is extremely vulnerable to chemicals such as acetone found in many aerosol spray paints, nail polish remover, and some glues and will collapse it on contact.

Actually, Styrofoam isn't the correct name for the expanded polystyrene foam used in popular hot/cold drinking cups. Instead, Styrofoam is the official, trademark name for an extruded (not expanded) polystyrene product. As mentioned previously, extruded means the material is forced through an opening and shaped. It isn't expanded with gases.

Extrusion makes for a much heavier-duty product. Extruded polystyrene—true Styrofoam—is so strong that it is used in surfboards, life rafts, and in building insulation. We will continue with the term Styrofoam as it is commonly used, indicating the cups.

💡 Science Project Ideas

- Test different plastics found in the home to see if any dissolve in acetone. Those that are numbered with a Plastic Resin Identification Code (see Appendix B) can be identified by chemical name. Which tend to be more soluble in acetone, polymers with oxygen in them or polymers without oxygen?

- How much air is enclosed in a sample of Styrofoam? One way to find out is to first measure the volume of a block of Styrofoam. Then, measure the volume of the same block after it has been collapsed in acetone and dried. What problems do you see that might cause your results to be too high or too low? Explain.

- What polymer is used for the packaging of olive, sesame, canola, or corn oil used in cooking? The oils are all hydrocarbons. Will they dissolve polymers that are also hydrocarbons? Conduct experiments to find out whether any of the oils dissolve in polymeric hydrocarbons. The polymers that are hydrocarbon compounds most resembling cooking oils are Numbers 2, 4, and 5 in the Plastic Resin Identification Code (see Appendix B).

EXPERIMENT 2.5

Fabrics That Like Water, Fabrics That Don't

Question:

How does nylon fabric (made from hydrophobic polymers) compare with cotton fabric (natural materials)?

Hypothesis:

Nylon polymer will quickly shed water, while a natural fiber, such as cotton, will absorb water and stay wet.

Materials:

- square of cotton fabric
- square of nylon fabric
- water
- thin string
- 2 chairs
- scissors

Is cotton fabric hydrophilic or hydrophobic? That is: Is cotton a comparatively waterproof material, or is it a material that is easy to wet? What about nylon? The following brief experiment offers a simple test to find out.

Procedure:

1. Make a short clothesline by tying a length of thin string from one chair to another.

2. Cut out one nylon square and one cotton square of fabric, both equal in size. Try to find fabrics that are used for the same purpose, such as for undershirts, so that they are woven similarly.

Figure 15.

Two fabric samples are hung to dry.

3. Place each of the fabrics in water until soaked. Lift each from the water and hold it briefly until dripping slows.

4. Fold each separately over the string so that they are hanging the same way as shown in Figure 15. Observe how long each takes to dry. Based on your observations, is either one hydrophilic?

Results and Conclusions

The fabric that dries much more slowly is hydrophilic, while the one that dries rapidly is hydrophobic.

Nylon is a hydrophobic polymer that is manufactured as a fiber that can be woven into cloth, carpets, and rope. Since nylon doesn't like water, it resists getting wet and won't absorb or hold water. This means it won't deteriorate as quickly as natural fibers, such as cotton, which soaks up water and retains moisture. This makes nylon more durable, since moisture can make natural material rot over time. Nylon is strong enough to be used in many types of tires and in parachutes.

Science Project Ideas

- It is evident from Experiment 2.5 that cotton is made up of polymers that attract water whereas nylon has comparatively little attraction for water. Look up the structure of water in a chemistry book. Also, find out the structures of nylon and of cotton. Based on these structures, develop a hypothesis to explain why nylon is hydrophobic and cotton is hydrophilic. You may need to ask someone knowledgeable in chemistry to help you.

- Test other natural and synthetic fibers to determine whether they are hydrophilic or hydrophobic. Develop a hypothesis to explain differences in behavior.

- Compare fabrics made of nylon and of polypropylene to see which is more hydrophobic. Be careful to keep all variables under control, such as the thickness of the fiber and the type and closeness of the weave, and the amount of water left in the fabric before hanging.

EXPERIMENT 2.6

Permeability to Water

Question:

Do all food wraps made of polymers function equally?

Hypothesis:

The ability of various popular food wraps to retain moisture varies according to the polymers used in their manufacture.

Materials:

- low-density polyethyl-ene food wrap (Saran Premium Wrap and either Handiwrap or Glad Wrap)
- polyvinyl chloride food wrap (Reynold's Plastic Wrap or "stretch-tite")
- measuring cup
- scissors
- water
- 4 drinking glasses, all the same size
- 3 identical rubber bands
- 3 labels
- pen
- box

How well does food wrap (plastic wrap) keep foods moist? How well does it keep outside moisture from getting in? A covering that allows water molecules to pass through it is said to be permeable to water. This experiment will test three different food wraps, or films, for their permeability to water vapor.

Procedure:

1. Label three drinking glasses as follows: "PE" for the polyethylenes Handiwrap or Glad Wrap, "PVC" for the polyvinyl chloride Reynold's Plastic Wrap, and "Saran" for Saran Premium Wrap, another type of polyethylene wrap.

2. Add ¾ cup of water to a measuring cup. Pour the water into one glass and allow the cup to drain into it for 5 seconds.

3. Repeat for the next two glasses, measuring and pouring as carefully alike as you can for all three glasses. Repeat for the unlabeled fourth drinking glass.

4. Cut one square of each film to fit over a glass. Each square should be the same size.

5. Start with the glass labeled "PE" and cover it with Handiwrap or Glad Wrap. Make sure the film fits snugly, but try not to stretch it. Put a rubber band tightly around the glass to hold the film down.

6. Repeat with the appropriate films for the other two labeled glasses, carefully doing them in the same way as for the first glass, as shown in Figure 16.

7. Place all three glasses plus the open, unlabeled glass of water together in an open box and place the box at the back of a closet.

Figure 16.

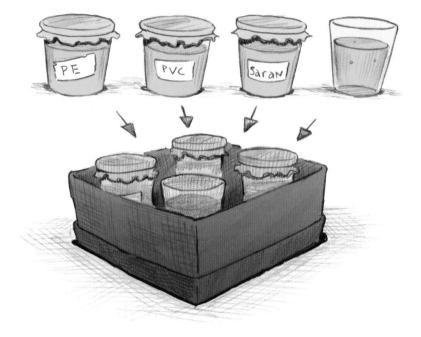

Cover the three glasses, which are partially filled with water, with plastic wrap. Leave the fourth cup uncovered.

Your purpose is to keep the four glasses undisturbed and at the same temperature during the experiment. By keeping all the variables the same except for the two variables that you are investigating—termed controlling the variables—you can compare the permeabilities of the three films. The two variables are: a) the different types of film, and b) how much water evaporates from each glass.

8. Every few days examine the three glasses to compare the levels of water in them. Continue until you can place the three glasses in order, from greatest loss of water to least loss of water, or until you conclude that all three remain unchanged over several weeks.

Results and Conclusions

How much water, if any, was lost from each glass? Use the measuring cup to find out. Be sure to dry the measuring cup between measurements and to drain each glass for the same period of time.

What are your conclusions? What is the purpose of testing the glass of water with no cover on it? That glass of water is called an "experimental control."

Which film is most permeable to water? What about the other two? How does the water loss in the covered glasses compare to that of the glass with no cover on it?

The permeability of various food wraps differs, but their properties also vary. This influences how people choose one wrap or another. One purpose of enclosing food in plastic wrap is to keep in moisture during freezing. When food is kept frozen for extended periods it can lose moisture, resulting in the condition known as "freezer burn." Some wraps are preferred for commercial purposes, while others are favored for household use.

For example, the polyvinyl chloride wrap stretches and clings extremely well and is preferred for commercial purposes, but there are questions about harmful chemicals in the material. Low density polyethylenes (such as Saran Premium Wrap, Handiwrap, and Glad Wrap) may not seal as tightly as polyvinyl chloride and so are more permeable. However, they may not contain such potentially harmful added chemicals.

Science Project Ideas

- Which food wrap of those available in the local store provides the best protection from oxygen in the air, that is, which is impermeable to oxygen? To find out, some kind of indicator is needed to show when oxygen has passed through the film. A slice of apple is very convenient for this purpose, since the flesh discolors on exposure to the oxygen in the air. Keep in mind that it is important to control all the variables except the two that you are testing. The apple slices will start discoloring as soon as exposed to air, so be sure to prepare the slices and to enclose them all at the same time. Which provides better protection, wrapping the apple slice completely with film or placing it in a glass and covering the glass with film? In Experiment 2.5, an uncovered glass of water was used as a control. What will you use for this investigation? Compare your results to those of Experiment 2.5.

- Are the results obtained in Experiment 2.5 the same when the temperature changes? One way to control the temperature is to carry out the experiment in a refrigerator that is usually kept closed. Compare the permeabilities of the food wraps at the refrigerator temperature. How does permeability to water change with temperature? Carry out a similar experiment for permeability to oxygen.

- Television commercials about food wraps often claim that their product provides the best seal to itself. Devise and carry out an experiment to test how well each wrap sticks to itself. State the variables that you controlled and how you did it. Indicate whether there were variables that you could not control and how these affected the outcomes. Is there a difference between the ability of a wrap to cling to itself and to cling to a glass surface? Does this affect the useful- ness of the wrap? What are your conclusions?

- Test how well different food wraps cling to a container. Does the material out of which the container is made make a difference? Does it make a difference if the outside of the container is wet?

CHAPTER 3

Testing Plastics

Beginning in the 1950s, the manufacture of plastics began to change from a minor industrial process to a major part of the worldwide economy. Plastics were developed to meet all kinds of needs, and the use of every type of polymer multiplied. This resulted in a totally new problem: plastic pollution. The accumulation of plastics in the garbage became frightening. Landfills grew uncontrollably when the plastics and wax-coated paper in them failed to decay. Piles of plastics were found floating in the middle of the oceans, trapping fish and bringing pollution. There was clearly a need for some way to reduce the pollution. Environmentalists called for regulations to control this growth of plastics.

It was then that serious thought was given to recycling. Before re-use of the plastic materials could take the place, the plastic trash had to be separated.

◄ Plastic bottles hold drinking water, but when empty they create large quantities of plastic waste.

Unfortunately, there were so many different plastics that there was no easy, inexpensive way to do this. A decision was reached internationally, a decision of the utmost importance. It was decided to greatly cut back on the number of materials used in packaging. Code numbers from <1> to <6> were assigned to the chosen plastics. The numbers, set inside a triangle made of bent arrows, were to be placed somewhere on each plastic product. The number <7> was chosen for a category in which to lump all the plastics used for special packaging not covered by the first six categories. Compliance with this scheme by the manufacturers was voluntary.

Town by town, village by village, city by city, the entire United States began to cooperate to help recycle plastics. Residents and businesses separated their plastics into bins according to the local rules and set them out for pickup. In many places, homeowners and businesses paid for the waste collectors to pick up garbage and plastics separately. In other places, the local government paid for it. Little by little, the frightening wave of plastic pollution began to decrease. It was a major victory.

Plastics have brought us an abundance of benefits, but every plus carries some minuses with it. Watchfulness must not be relaxed in the fight against plastic pollution, and the cooperation between manufacturers and consumers must continue. Only in this way can we all gain in the benefits brought to us by plastics.

EXPERIMENT 3.1

Identification and Separation of Plastics for Recycling

Question:

Are there tests that can tell the difference between the differently coded plastics for recycling?

Hypothesis:

Yes. Different tests can be performed to separate one type of plastic from another.

The technique in this experiment uses materials generally available in the home or local store. It was developed by the American Plastics Council.

The list of used plastics (also called resins) that are picked up for recycling or disposal may be found in Appendix B. Note that there are two kinds of polyethylene listed: low density polyethylene (LDPE) and high density polyethylene (HDPE).

LDPE is made under conditions that cause extensive cross-linking to occur. As a result, the chains can't get close to each other. Because the chains are farther apart, the density of the polyethylene is lowered. HDPE, on the other hand, is made to produce long chains without cross-linking. These chains tend to line up close to each other causing this polymer to be denser than LDPE.

It is always a good idea to first try out a set of tests using "knowns," that is, samples whose identities (properties) are known. That is what you can do

Materials:

- **an adult**
- 1 sample each of plastics numbered <2>, <4>, and <5> (see Appendix B)
- 2 samples each of plastics numbered <1>, <3>, and <6>
- finger-sized strip of PET (code <1>) cut from a 2-liter soda bottle
- cup or bowl of water
- clean wooden craft or popsicle sticks
- paper towels
- safety goggles
- 100 mL graduated cylinder or household glass or metal measuring cup
- isopropyl alcohol (70 percent)
- sink with running water
- Mazola corn oil
- copper wire 23–30 cm (9–12 in) long and about the thickness of the wire used for a No. 1 paper clip
- flame from stove burner or Bunsen burner
- cork, large size
- cookie sheet or other flat metal pan
- tongs
- acetone
- drinking glass
- scissors
- pot

next. Carry out the test on samples cut from empty containers marked with the recycling code number. Cut out one sample of each plastic listed in Appendix B (recycling codes <1> through <6>). A sample about the size of a large aspirin pill is satisfactory. The sample shouldn't have a label or writing on it since that may change the density. The shape isn't important, so you can use shape to help identify the sample for yourself. If a sample is difficult to cut, be sure to **have an adult** help you. A thicker sample is better than a thin one; so do not use food wrap.

In Figure 17, the steps and choices in the identification process are charted. The chart is an excellent aide to consult at any time during the experiment.

Figure 17.

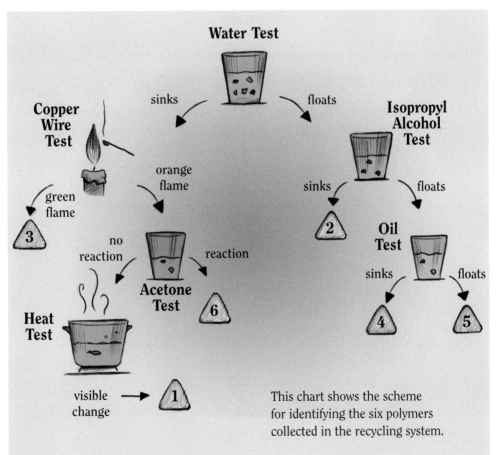

This chart shows the scheme for identifying the six polymers collected in the recycling system.

Water Density Test Procedure:

1. Fill a cup or bowl with water and let it stand a while to reach room temperature.

2. Put one of the samples into it. Poke the sample with a clean wooden craft stick or popsicle stick to knock off any bubbles on it that might cause it to float.

3. Add the other five samples and poke them similarly. Three samples should float, and three should sink as shown in Figure 18.

4. Remove the samples that float and dry them. Set them aside on a paper towel marked to identify them.

5. Remove the samples that sink, dry them, and set them aside on another paper towel marked to indicate that they sink.

The samples that float are less dense than water. The samples that sink are denser than water. Based on Table 2, identify the samples that floated.

Safety: *Wear goggles during the remainder of this experiment.*

Figure 18.

During the water density test, three samples will float and three will sink.

Samples That Float in Water
Isopropyl Alcohol Test Procedure:

1. Obtain 70 percent isopropyl alcohol (also called isopropanol) from the supermarket or drugstore (do not use any other percentage).

   Safety: *Isopropyl alcohol is flammable, so be sure to use it in a well-ventilated area away from any flame, and keep it covered.*

2. Pour 60 g (65 mL or 2.6 fl oz) of 70 percent isopropyl alcohol into a graduated cylinder or glass or metal measuring cup.

3. Add enough water to make 100 mL (4 fl oz) in all.

   This has to be done very carefully and is best done using graduated cylinders for measurements.

4. Mix well with a clean wooden craft or popsicle stick.

Table 2.
Density of Polymers in Recycling Scheme

Abbreviation	Name	Density
H_2O	Water	1.00
(1) PET	Polyethylene terephthalate	1.38–1.39
(2) HDPE	High density polyethylene	0.95–0.97
(3) PVC	Polyvinyl chloride	1.16–1.35
(4) LDPE	Low density polyethylene	0.92–0.94
(5) PP	Polypropylene	0.90–0.91
(6) PS	Polystyrene	1.05–1.07

5. If measured with a graduated cylinder, pour the alcohol solution into a drinking glass.

6. Place all three of the samples that floated into the alcohol solution.

7. Poke each sample with a wooden stick to push it under the surface and dislodge any air bubbles on the sample. One sample will sink. Based on their densities, which sample sinks?

   The sample that sinks is the one that is the densest of the three samples. It is high-density polyethylene (HDPE), code <2>.

8. Remove the HDPE sample, dry it, and discard it along with the wooden sticks into the waste bin.

9. Remove the two samples that floated and dry them for the next test. Pour the isopropanol down the sink and run water after it for half a minute.

Oil Test Procedure:

1. Fill a drinking glass (not plastic) half full of Mazola corn oil. No other oil may be substituted since it may have a different density.

2. Place the two unidentified samples into the oil. Poke each with a wooden stick to be sure bubbles are bumped off it. One sample will slowly sink and the other will end up floating. What is the name of the sample that sinks? What is the name of the sample that floats?

3. Discard the oil into a covered container and throw it away.

4. Dry the samples and discard them along with the sticks into the waste bin.

Samples That Sink in Water
Copper Wire Test Procedure:

Note: Polyvinyl chloride is usually not recycled so you may choose to skip this test. However, you may need to know how to do the test in order to identify an unknown plastic.

Adult supervision is required for this test.

1. Place one of the three samples that sank onto a cookie sheet or other flat metal pan.

Figure 19.

The Copper Wire Test

2. Obtain a copper wire 23 to 30 cm (9 to 12 in) in length.

3. Holding a large cork firmly on a desk with one hand, twist one end of the wire partway into the cork so that you can use the cork to lift the wire.

   For the remainder of this test, do not touch the wire with your fingers. **Always use the cork to move the wire.**

4. **Have an adult** turn on the flame.

5. Place the exposed tip of the wire into the upper part of the flame as shown in Figure 19.

6. When the wire tip is red-hot, remove it from the flame and quickly touch the tip to the sample so as to melt some plastic. Then, quickly lift off the wire so that a bit of plastic sticks to it.

7. Place the wire tip with the plastic on it back into the tip of the flame and observe the flame while you are holding it there.

   A green color will identify PVC, polyvinyl chloride, code <3>. An orange color in the flame is a negative result. Place the cork on the metal sheet until the wire is cool.

8. If the test is positive, you may go on to the next step. Otherwise, start again by heating the tip of the wire in the flame.

9. Check the remaining two samples in the same way as the first one. One of them should give a positive test.

   The samples not identified so far are PS and PET.

Acetone Test Procedure:

You will need to use new samples of PS and PET.

Safety: *Acetone is flammable and should be used only where no flame is near. Because it evaporates readily, use it only in a well-ventilated room or outdoors. Wear safety goggles whenever you work with acetone. Keep any container of acetone tightly covered when not in use. You may wish to wear plastic gloves because acetone dries the skin. A little hand cream will remoisturize your skin. Small quantities of acetone may be safely disposed down the sink, but be sure to wash it down with running water for at least 30 seconds.*

1. Pour acetone into a drinking glass until one-fourth full.

2. With tongs, place the two unidentified samples under the acetone until one of them turns whitish.

3. Remove the whitened sample with the tongs and hold it for a few seconds to drip dry.

4. Press the sample firmly with your fingers. The polymer may feel softer and a little sticky. With your fingernail, try to scrape off some of the plastic from the surface.

   If the sample whitens, or feels softened, or if you can scrape it a bit, this is a positive result that identifies polystyrene (PS), code <6>. The other sample should be unchanged.

5. Continue to the last confirming test, which should be used on both samples.

Heat Test Procedure:

This test is more dramatic if you cut a strip from a 2-liter soda bottle. The bottle is made of PET.

Adult supervision is required for this test.

1. Place a pot of water on the stove and heat it to gentle boiling. Make sure the pot doesn't dry. Use tongs to grasp the sample to be tested.

2. Place it into boiling water. You can expect to see a surprising change. The change is a positive test for polyethylene terephthalate (PET), code <1>.

3. You may discard the remaining samples into the waste bin.

Results and Conclusions

This separation scheme should have identified each of your samples correctly. Sometimes, as mentioned earlier, the presence of additives in the plastics may have altered the properties of the plastic to give a misleading result. For recycling purposes, this system is still satisfactory.

Try this scheme on a sample of a plastic container that doesn't have the code number. Can it be identified? What problems were encountered, and how did you resolve them?

In order to reprocess plastic, the recycling manufacturer needs to know what kind of plastic it is. Identifying the plastic will tell how it is affected by such things as oil, water, certain chemicals, and heat.

There are several ways to separate and identify the six plastics in the recycling system. The tests just used are not conclusive because the addition of additives to the polymer to form the plastic can alter the responses to the tests. However, these tests are extremely useful as a guide to separating polymers for recycling.

Science Project Ideas

- Invent a new scheme to separate the six packaging materials in the recycling process by making solutions of different densities that will help the separations. You may use materials available in a high school laboratory if you obtain the cooperation of your chemistry teacher. For your process to be industrially accepted, the materials to be used for the separations should not be expensive and must be safe to use. Write complete instructions and construct a flow chart like the one in Figure 17.

- How successful has the recycling program been? How well has it carried out its original purpose? Has it failed in some ways? Prepare a report on this and include your assessment of its success.

- Are plastic spoons and forks made out of recyclable material? Usually, they are not marked because there is no convenient space for a mark. Test both the white and the transparent spoons or forks using the scheme in Experiment 3.1 to identify them.

EXPERIMENT 3.2

Measuring the Stretch

Question:

Plastic wraps are made to be elastic, but do they stretch equally in all directions?

Hypothesis:

The process of manufacturing plastic wrap determines in which direction the wrap is more stretchable.

Materials:

- roll of plastic film used to wrap foods
- permanent ink marker
- tape measure
- scissors
- friend

The thin plastic films used for food wraps can usually be stretched. How far do they stretch? Do they stretch more in one direction than in another? Do they shrink back to the original size? This experiment will investigate these questions using a plastic film of your choice. Having a friend to help will make the preparations and measurements much easier.

Procedure:

1. Unroll some plastic film. Be careful not to stretch any of the film as you work with it. Most films used for food wrap are about 30 cm (12 in) from side to side.

2. Cut a strip from one side to the other that is about 3 cm (1¼ in) wide (see Figure 20).

Figure 20.

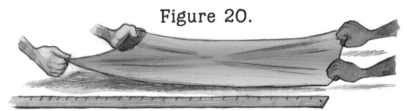

Measure a piece of plastic wrap before and after stretching.

3. Label the strip "W" for "Width" with permanent ink. Cut and label two other such strips. It is important that you cut all strips with smooth, straight edges.

4. Gently extend the roll until you have pulled out a length of about 30 cm (12 in). Cut a strip about 3 cm (1¼ in) wide up the long side of the film and label it "L" for "Length."

5. Cut a second strip of the same size in the same way and also label that "L."

6. Place one of the W strips so it lies smoothly on the table. Measure how long it is. Keep the tape measure along the long side of the strip while you extend the tape measure to make it at least twice as long as the strip.

7. Ask your friend to gradually stretch the film along the tape with a steady pull until the strip breaks. Note how long the strip was before it broke. Repeat, but this time stretch the film only about 5 cm (2 in)

before releasing it. How long is it after it is released? Did it go back to the original length?

8. Repeat the stretching and measuring with the second strip of W film until it breaks. Be careful to stretch the film at the same speed as before. Average the two results.

9. Now, repeat the entire process with the two strips of L film.

Results and Conclusions

Which stretched more, film from the width or film from the length of the roll? Compare the elasticity of each strip, that is, how close to its original length it came after moderate stretching.

💡 Science Project Ideas

- Use the method of Experiment 3.2 to test the stretchability and elasticity at different orientations of various types of plastics used for packaging, such as food bags, garbage bags, and supermarket packing bags. Also test Reynolds Food Wrap (polyvinyl chloride) and Saran Premium Wrap (low density polyethylene).

- How does temperature affect the stretchability of a food wrap? The elasticity?

- How is the stretchability and elasticity of a food wrap affected when it is stretched out over a wet counter top? How might this affect its use?

- Invent a method to measure the tensile strength of a plastic wrap. The tensile strength measures the weight needed to break apart a given strip of plastic wrap by

The difference in directional stretching is due to the manufacturing process, when the film was pulled along its length. As a result of the lengthwise pulling, the long polymer chains line themselves up along the length of the roll. The bonds between the atoms in the chains are quite strong, so the chains are difficult to stretch any further. Attractions between the chains, however, are quite weak. When the film is pulled along its width, the chains can be pulled away from each other. As a result, it is much easier to stretch the film along its width than its length before the film breaks.

pulling on it. This differs from the length to which the film stretches before breaking. The weight needed can be obtained by hanging a bag from the bottom of a vertical strip held at its top and adding water or beans or steel balls or other materials that can be weighed until the strip breaks. Submit your plan for approval to a responsible adult or science teacher before carrying it out. Compare different brands of the same type of film, such as food wrap or trash bags, to see which has the greatest tensile strength. Are there differences? Why? Explain why tensile strength is important for this product.

- Does the direction of the pull on a plastic, whether along the length or width, make a difference in the tensile strength? Investigate and report on it for a variety of different films.

EXPERIMENT 3.3

Shrink Wraps

Question:

How do commercial plastic wraps shrink to enclose products?

Hypothesis:

Some plastics shrink when heated, allowing them to form a tight seal around a product.

Materials:

- **an adult**
- scissors
- 3 thin, transparent food containers labeled code <6>, each having a flat surface in it such as a supermarket salad container, plastic bakery box, and/or
- lid from a yogurt container
- ruler
- fine-tip permanent pen
- aluminum foil
- oven
- oven mitts
- heat resistant surface such as the top of the stove

How does a manufacturer get plastic to wrap tightly around a product? Shrink wrap does the job. Although shrink wrap isn't sold in retail stores, there are other types of plastics available for experimentation that shrink when heated.

Procedure:

1. Obtain three thin, transparent food containers marked code <6> (see suggestions under *Materials*), each with a flat surface in it.

2. Cut a flat rectangular piece from each of these, about 10 cm (4 in) x 5 cm (2 in). If you can't find three different containers, take extra samples from what you have.

3. With permanent marking pen, place a number or letter on each rectangle to identify it. Keep records of the markings and of all the measurements that you take.

4. Measure the length and width of each rectangle.

5. **With adult supervision,** heat the oven to 355°F.

6. Space the rectangles apart from each other on a sheet of aluminum foil.

7. Wearing oven mitts, place the foil with samples on it into the oven and close the door.

8. After five minutes, wearing the oven mitts, remove the foil with the plastic samples from the oven. Place the foil on a heat-resistant surface. Allow it to cool completely.

9. Measure the length and width of each sample after cooling.

Results and Conclusions

Did all the samples shrink to the same size in length? In width? Do you see any other changes? What was the percent change in length and the percent change in width for each sample? You can calculate the percent from the following formula, first for length and then for width.

$$\frac{\text{amount of the decrease in length}}{\text{original length}} \times 100\% = \text{percent change in length}$$

The change may vary slightly from rectangle to rectangle if the heating in the oven is uneven.

The explanation for the shrinkage has to do with the way polystyrene sheets are shaped in the manufacture of the product. The polystyrene is heated, stretched out to a sheet, and then rapidly cooled.

The quick cooling fixes the long, stretched-out polymer chains in the shape they have at that moment. When the plastic is heated in the oven, the chains gain the energy to become free again, and return to their shorter, unstretched shape. Since the sheet has been pulled more in the length than the width, the percent of change by heating is greater in the length.

💡 Science Project Ideas

- Investigate whether there is also a change in weight when shrinkable polystyrene is heated.

- Compare the shrinkage of flat rectangular samples of the same shrinkable polystyrene container at different oven temperatures. Try starting at 250°F and increasing the temperature by 35°F each time, measuring the change in size as in Experiment 3.3. Hypothesize an explanation of what you observe.

- Does the thickness of a sample affect the shrinkage?

- How long do plastics last in the environment? Collect several different paper cups and several different plastic cups. To make comparisons, these should all be similar in size and shape. Bury each of these separately in the soil outdoors. Once each month, dig them all up and examine their condition. When you have accumulated enough information to reach a conclusion, even if tentative, construct a report on your findings. Extend this project to test additional kinds of plastics.

EXPERIMENT 3.4

Heat Insulation

Question:

Which cups work best as insulators for hot drinks?

Hypothesis:

Cups made with expanded polystyrene, which contains air bubbles, will keep drinks hot longer than will hard plastic or paper cups.

Materials:

- 3 or more 10-oz hot-drink cups, all of similar diameter and height. One cup should be Styrofoam, one should be polystyrene or another plastic, and one should be paper.
- measuring cup
- hot sink water
- sink
- scissors
- candy thermometer (alcohol-based, sold in some hardware stores and craft stores)
- clock
- pencil and paper

This experiment will show which type of cup is the best thermal (heat) insulator, or will best keep a hot liquid from cooling off.

Procedure:

1. Obtain three or more 10-oz cups (see *Materials*). You may have to cut the top off a cup to make it the same height as the others.

2. Allow hot water from the faucet to flow until it is quite hot. Fill a measuring cup with the hot water and let it stand to heat up the cup itself.

3. Put the candy thermometer into the measuring cup in such a way that the weight of the thermometer won't tip the cup over.

4. After a minute, remove the thermometer and hold it in your hand.

5. Pour out the water and immediately refill with hot water to the 1-cup level.

6. Quickly empty the water into one of the cups being tested.

7. Place the candy thermometer into the cup so that it stands safely. **Safety:** *Prop the cup if needed to prevent it from tipping. If the thermometer shows that the temperature is still rising, wait until it is steady.* Read the thermometer and record the reading.

8. Each minute after that, stir the water once with the thermometer and read the temperature without removing the thermometer from the cup. Continue for a total of twelve minutes, writing down your observations.

9. Remove the candy thermometer.

10. Discard the hot water.

Figure 21.
Time-Temperature Graph for Cooling Water in Cups of Different Compositions

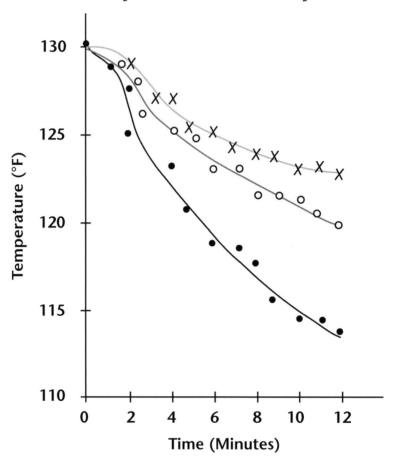

In the graph, the *x*- and *y*-axis need to be labeled and marked with appropriate values. The graph curves shown are each smooth lines that come as close to the data points as they can. Data points are shown by Xs, circles, and filled circles respectively. Your graph lines will probably not be identical in shape with the ones shown here. Based on your experiment, which of these curves is Styrofoam?

11. Repeat the above for each of the cups. Be sure that the timing for each starts at the same hot water temperature. Stir in the same way each time.

12. Draw time-temperature graphs for each cup. They all can be placed on one chart. See Figure 21 for an example.

Results and Conclusions

Which of the cups provided the best thermal insulation—that is, cooled the least in twelve minutes? Which of the cups was the worst insulator? How does plastic compare to paper?

Note that the paper cup probably had a wax or plastic coating over it to help make it waterproof.

Expanded polystyrene foam, generally known as Styrofoam, is manufactured using a "gaseous blowing agent." This process creates the air pockets that make the material spongy and a good thermal insulator. Air pockets keep warmth in and cold out, insulating the liquid.

💡 Science Project Ideas

- Now that you have experience with testing for heat insulation, devise an experiment to test the insulating properties of different polymers. Identify each of the plastics that is tested. Discuss how the variables are controlled and which, if any, were not able to be controlled. Make a chart comparing the results of your work.

- How important is the presence of air in Styrofoam to its insulating qualities? Devise an experiment to carefully compare the insulating qualities of Styrofoam and polystyrene.

- How important is the thickness of the plastic to its ability to insulate? How does the insulating ability change with the thickness of the container? Conduct experiments to find out.

- A property that is important to industry but that has not been tested in this chapter is the impact strength of a film, that is, how the material responds to an object dropping onto it. This is called a falling dart test. For your test, devise a way to tightly hold a film of plastic stretched out. For example, the film might be stretched over the top of a coffee can and held in place with a thick rubber band. For the dart, small balls of different weight can be used. The variables you will need to test to find out the impact strength needed to break the film include the type of film (such as food wrap, grocery bags, dry-cleaner garment bags, and supermarket bags), the weight of the dart, and the height of the drop. Keep in mind that only two variables may change during each experiment.

- What happens to the impact strength of a sample of film after it has been previously tested without breaking?

CHAPTER 4

The Mysterious Case of Natural Rubber

Natural rubber was probably the first elastic material discovered by humans. The early Indians of South and Central America made rubber balls for sports. As early as the 1700s, rubber was used to rub out pencil marks, a use that gave rubber its name. Natural rubber comes from a milky liquid called latex found in the stems of some plants. The great rubber plantations harvest their latex from a tree originally found in the Amazon valley, *Hevea brasiliensis*. You can, if you wish, get your own latex from goldenrod or dandelion plants. Simply rub the white liquid from a broken stem between your fingers, and you will soon have a tiny ball of rubber.

◄ A bucket is positioned to catch the latex sap from a rubber tree.

Charles Goodyear (1800–1860) was very interested in rubber. His interest began after the "rubber fever" in the early 1830s suddenly ended. It ended because the exciting new gum from a tree in Brazil that could be used to make balls and waterproof products turned out to be a mess. It melted in the summer and became stiff and hard in the winter. Investors in the new product lost many millions. Goodyear started experimenting with rubber, hoping to improve its properties. Although he was a bankrupt inventor at the time, he nevertheless spent his time trying to make rubber into a satisfactory waterproof solid for both winter and summer temperatures. After five years, he still had not conquered the problem. He was so poor by then that his children were reduced to eating donations of milk and potatoes obtained from local farmers.

It was in 1839 in Massachusetts that Goodyear made his great discovery. On a cold day in February, he is said to have again gone into the general store to show off his latest product to the men gathered there. This time, the rubber was supposedly improved by the addition of sulfur. The sticky gum he displayed was met with snickers. Goodyear became upset and, in his anger, waved the gum in the air. As he did so, the gum flew out of his fingers and landed on a hot potbellied stove. When Goodyear went to scrape the blob of rubber off the stove, it was remarkably changed. Instead of melting, it had charred in the middle with a brown springy rim around the outside. The bouncy rim was pliable at high and low temperatures and waterproof.

Commercial success did not come to Goodyear quickly or easily. Goodyear developed a process based on the added sulfur, which he called vulcanization, and patented the process in 1844. He struggled to produce a saleable product but made bad business deals. He had to fight patent infringement cases in court but, even so, was honored by some. When he died, he was heavily in debt. Today, rubber production and manufacture is a multimillion dollar industry.

Although the potbellied stove discovery has often been described in history as a mere accident, Goodyear always said that it was more than that. What happened with the blob on the stove had meaning, said he, only for that person "whose mind was prepared to draw an inference." An accident such as that can happen at any time, but a great discovery can be made only by one who sees what it means.

This chapter will present some of the unique properties of polymers. You will examine the behaviors of some polymers used in the home. As you go through the experiments, you will find that the unique properties of polymers provide clues to why vulcanization changed the properties of natural rubber so drastically. Your challenge is to put all the clues together to solve this mystery. The case isn't easy to solve. Good luck!

EXPERIMENT 4.1

Making a Plastic Fiber

Question:

Can a synthetic polymer be made into a fiber?

Hypothesis:

By dissolving the water in a polymer mix, a fiber will be formed.

Materials:

- Elmer's Washable School Glue
- glass rod or pencil
- acetone
- very small container made of glass, metal, or plastic
- toothpicks
- safety goggles
- sink with running water
- paper towel

This experiment will demonstrate one way to make a synthetic fiber from a synthetic polymer. The industrial process is called cold drawing. The experiment calls for the use of acetone, which may be purchased in the paint section of hardware stores.

Safety: *Acetone is flammable and should be used only where no flame is near. Because it evaporates readily, use it only in a well-ventilated room or outdoors. Wear safety goggles whenever you work with acetone. Keep any container of acetone tightly covered when not in use. You may wish to wear plastic gloves because it dries the skin. A little hand cream will remoisturize your skin.*

Elmer's Washable School Glue, which is used in this experiment, is a solution of a hydrophilic polymer with a carbon backbone (polyvinyl acetate). The glue also contains some water and other ingredients needed to improve its effectiveness.

Procedure:

1. Obtain a small container such as a cap on a spray can or metal bottle cap or a very small glass.

2. Put on your safety goggles.

3. Pour a little acetone into the container to check that the acetone doesn't damage it. Select a different container if this happens.

4. Pour the used acetone into the sink, run water after it for about thirty seconds, and dry the container with a paper towel.

5. Pour Elmer's Washable glue into your container to a height of about 1 cm (⅓ in). Dip one end of a toothpick into the glue and try to lift a strand out of it with the aid of the toothpick. You will find that the glue flows off the toothpick.

You will need a glass rod for the next part of this experiment. If you cannot obtain a rod, you may substitute a pencil.

6. Any paint on the pencil should be removed by using acetone-moistened paper towels. **Safety:** *Be sure that no flame is nearby when you do this. Allow the paper to air-dry in a well-ventilated location before discarding it.*

7. Tilt the container a bit and carefully pour an equal height of acetone over the glue.

8. With the glass rod nearby, lower the point of the toothpick into the container until it is where the two layers meet as shown in Figure 22. Use the toothpick to gently lift a bit of the lower layer upward in the form of a strand. It may take a little practice to get this to work, and you may have to pull out a clump to get it started.

9. When you have one end of an unbroken strand (fiber) lifted above the container, bring the glass rod over to it and lay the fiber around it. Keep the rod slightly above the container because the wet fiber is weak and will break if extended.

10. Carefully wind the fiber in a spiral around the rod. With practice, you will find that you can wind the spiral along the entire length of the rod.

11. Rinse the little container thoroughly with water. Remove the goggles. The fiber can be allowed to dry on the rod in a well-ventilated location. When dry, you can unwind it from the rod.

Results and Conclusions

Acetone was used in this experiment because water is very soluble in it. The acetone dissolves the water in the polymer mix as the polymer is drawn from the solution, allowing the fiber to form.

Figure 22.

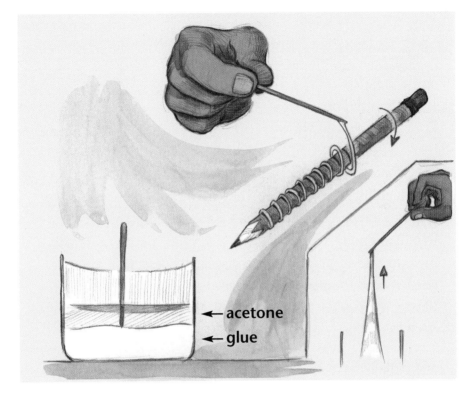

acetone

glue

Pass a toothpick through the acetone to where the acetone and glue layers meet.

Nylon fibers for fabrics and ropes are made by cold drawing in a process similar to the one in this experiment. However, nylon is made by reacting two different monomers. One monomer is in the upper layer, and the other is in the lower layer. The reaction takes place at the interface where the two layers meet.

A unique property of some polymers is that the tangled chains can be pulled, twisted, and spun into long, continuous fibers. Many products are made from synthetic fibers. Fabrics are made by weaving fibers together into different patterns. In earlier times, these fibers were spun of natural polymers, mostly wool, cotton, silk, and flax. Today, around the world, cotton is still the chief fiber produced, but synthetics run a close second.

Science Project Ideas

- Test the dry glue fibers produced in Experiment 4.1 for stretchability. How far do they stretch compared to the original length? Do they snap back after stretching? Produce enough fiber to weave a small patch of fabric. Include this in your project display. Would this make a good fabric for family use? Discuss the pros and cons. Would it be good for insulation? How would you find out? Test it and give your method and conclusion.

- Try the method of cold drawing used in Experiment 4.1 with other water-soluble glues to see if a fiber can be drawn.

EXPERIMENT 4.2

Hydrocarbons and Microwaves

Question:
Are polystyrene food containers safe to use in a microwave?

Hypothesis:
If a polystyrene food container holding water undergoes change when heated in the microwave, it won't be safe to use for food.

Materials:
- **an adult**
- 2 transparent or translucent polystyrene cups (code <6> in the recycling system; see Appendix B)
- microwave oven
- safety goggles
- paper plate
- sink water

What happens when a solid polymer is heated? Experiments 4.2 and 4.3 will examine this.

A microwave oven heats food largely by heating the water in the food. In effect, the water is boiled from the outside in. Since the water in the food is heated to its boiling point (100°C, 212°F), the container chosen to hold the food should not sag or melt at the boiling point of water. Also, the container should not be made of a material that is itself heated by the microwave to where it can become dangerously hot or even melt. Polystyrene is a thermoplastic hydrocarbon and so won't be heated by the microwave. But is polystyrene absolutely safe to use in the microwave? You will check this.

An adult must supervise this experiment.

Procedure:

1. Obtain two transparent or translucent polystyrene cups.

2. Put on your safety goggles.

3. Place one empty cup into the microwave and operate the machine for 3 minutes at full power.

4. Remove the cup and inspect it. Set it aside. Is polystyrene the kind of material that heats up in a microwave?

5. Fill the other cup about one-fourth full of tap water. Place a paper plate into the microwave to catch any water that might spill out.

6. Put the cup of water into the microwave. If the machine has power levels, operate it at level seven (such machines usually, but not always, have higher wattages than those without power levels). Set the microwave for 3 minutes and start it.

7. Watch carefully through the microwave window throughout. If at any time the cup appears to be leaking, shut off the microwave immediately, but keep the door closed. **Safety:** *You never want to open the microwave until the water is cooled.* When the water starts to boil, allow it to microwave for another minute and then shut off the power.

8. Allow the cup to cool for a minute or two before you open the door to look at the cup. **Safety:** *You must allow the water to cool to room temperature before you remove the cup from the microwave, probably 4 to 5 minutes.* Did the cup melt? Did you observe any part of it become liquid? What happened to the cup?

9. You can discard the water left in the cup. You may remove the goggles.

Results and Conclusions

Compare the cup that was heated with water to the one that was heated without water. When you are done with the cups, they may be discarded into the waste bin. Is it safe to heat water in a polystyrene cup?

The cup that was empty was not changed by the microwave. It may have warmed up a bit due to an additive in the plastic, or moisture trapped in the plastic during manufacture, or moisture on it from the air in the microwave. The cup that had water in it sagged and deformed as the water boiled, but only in the part that held water, as shown in Figure 23.

The cup did not melt. A melting cup would have formed some liquid, but this cup just changed shape. When removed from the microwave, it remained deformed and did not return to its original shape. It's concluded that it's not safe to microwave foods in a polystyrene container.

Figure 23.

The cup that had water in it sagged and deformed as the water boiled, but only in the part that held water. The cup did not melt.

Science Project Idea

- **With adult supervision, investigate containers numbered <1>, <2>, <4>, and <5> in the recycling system (see Appendix B) using the method of Experiment 4.2 to see whether they can be safely used to heat water in a microwave.**

EXPERIMENT 4.3

The Glass Transition Temperature

Question:

Does polystyrene melt in boiling water?

Hypothesis:

No, but heat can weaken polystyrene and cause it to sag.

Materials:

- **an adult**
- polystyrene cup (<6>); may be transparent or translucent, depending on the additives in it
- stove
- pot that holds at least 4 cups of liquid
- water
- table salt
- safety goggles
- large stainless steel soup ladle or slotted spoon
- oven mitts

Experiment 4.2 showed that boiling water in a polystyrene cup caused the cup to sag below the water level. Will the entire cup melt if it is covered by boiling water?

Procedure:

1. Place a 1- or 2-quart pot on the stove and fill it about ⅔ full of water. Once pure water boils, the temperature stays at 100°C (212°F) as long as there is any water present.

2. To obtain a slightly higher temperature, impurities may be added. For this purpose, add several tablespoons of salt to the water.

3. Put your goggles on. Place the polystyrene cup into the water. **Have an adult** heat the water to boiling, and **have the adult** continue to supervise the experiment until completed. Put on oven mitts.

4. As the water boils, gradually push the cup flat under the water as shown in Figure 24 with the aid of a stainless steel soup ladle or slotted spoon. Keep enough boiling water in the pot to cover the collapsed cup. Does the cup melt?

Figure 24.

Using a stainless steel soup ladle or slotted spoon, gradually push the cup flat under the water.

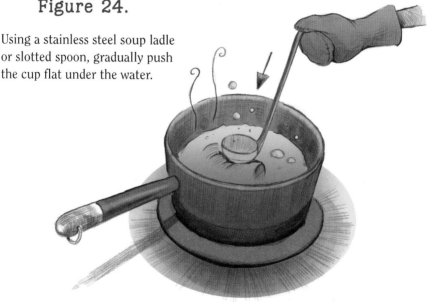

5. When the cup is collapsed, **ask an adult** to remove it from the hot water. Turn off the burner and allow the hot water to cool before pouring it out.

Results and Conclusions

Carefully inspect the cup. Did it melt? Can you pull it back into shape? You may remove your safety goggles.

Have you ever seen another solid behave this way? When other solids are heated up, they ordinarily melt and flow like melted ice or margarine, or they scorch, or even decompose (come apart chemically). They don't gradually sag without any liquid appearing.

The sagging and deforming of the cup that you observed is unique to certain polymers. The solid polymers that undergo the sagging are stiff and glassy below the temperature at which the change begins. Above that temperature, these solids become pliable, can be bent, and will give when pressed. The temperature at which the sagging takes place has a special name. It is called the glass transition temperature, abbreviated as T_g.

That is what happened with the polystyrene. Below its glass transition temperature, it was stiff and transparent or translucent. Once the T_g was reached, the polystyrene container became flexible and could be easily bent. When it was removed from the water, its temperature dropped to below the T_g, so it could no longer be reshaped.

Each polymer has its own T_g, which is partly dependent on how the polymer was made and on the additives and impurities in it.

💡 Science Project Ideas

- Polyvinyl acetate has a T_g of 28°C (about 82°F). It can be used to make a demonstration of the change in stiffness from glassy to rubbery near room temperature. Make a solid strip of the polymer from Elmer's Glue-All by pouring the glue into a plastic bowl and allowing the solvent to evaporate for several days. The additives in the glue may lower the T_g to perhaps 15 to 20°C. Cut a narrow strip of the polyvinyl acetate piece that you have made. Dip it into hot water and immediately twist it into a spiral. Allow it to cool. Dip this into ice water, and it will become glassy. Can it be untwisted? What happens when you put it back into hot water? Can it be twisted or straightened? To show your results as a display, exhibit the strips before and after each step, with an explanation. The viewer can touch the strips.

- Polymethyl methacrylate (a.k.a. Plexiglass, Lucite) is a typical glassy polymer. Find out what happens to it in a refrigerator, in a freezer, and in boiling water. Is there any indication of a change from glassy to rubbery at any of the temperatures? Try bending at each stage to observe whether there is any change. **An adult** must be present during the boiling water test. Explain the results.

- Obtain different balls that bounce at room temperature. Find out if the height of the bounce and the sound of the bounce is affected when at refrigerator temperature, freezer temperature, and when kept for a while in very hot water. If possible, examine the bounce in liquid nitrogen with adult supervision. What do you conclude about each T_g based on your observations?

- When polymers are prepared for commercial or industrial use, they usually have small quantities of different additives placed into them to improve them for the purposes needed. Thus, the nylon used to make fibers for stockings may be a little different from the nylon threads used for sewing or the nylon solid used in machine parts. Collect samples of several different products made of nylon. The T_g of pure nylon is about 50°C. With adult supervision of your experimental work, investigate the glass transition temperatures of the different nylon products. Note that the melting point of nylon isn't far above its T_g.

- Candles are usually made of paraffin, a mixture of chains with backbones of 18 to 36 carbon atoms and with hydrogen atoms at all the other bonds. The very long chain lengths put candle wax somewhat between ordinary hydrocarbon molecules and the shortest polymers (100 repeating units). Under adult supervision, find out whether candle wax has a glass transition temperature. If so, determine its approximate value.

◉EXPERIMENT 4.4

Elastomers

Question:

Can you make a rubber band out of rubber cement?

Hypothesis:

Yes. If the cement is carefully layered and allowed to dry between each layer, it will acquire an elastic consistency.

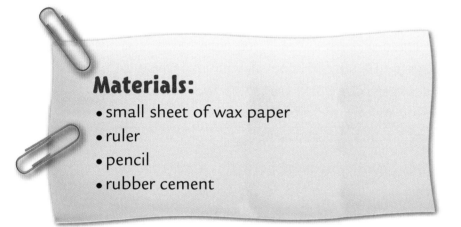

Materials:

- small sheet of wax paper
- ruler
- pencil
- rubber cement

Practically all synthetic substances that feel like hard rubber are polymers. They feel like rubber because they are above the T_g and can be depressed at least a bit. However, not all rubbers are highly elastic.

A highly elastic material can at least double or triple in length when pulled and then snap all the way back when released. Highly elastic materials are called elastomers. An elastomer is made of intertwined chains.

The chains elongate and line up when the elastomer is stretched, and snap back when it is released.

Unfortunately, natural rubber is an elastomer only at moderate temperatures. In hot weather, it becomes soft and sticky. In cold weather, it becomes hard and brittle. When Goodyear added sulfur to natural rubber, we know now that the sulfur cross-linked the polymer chains. Recall that cross-links are atoms or short chains of atoms that are bonded at each end to a different chain.

Figure 25a shows some chains of untreated natural rubber. Although not shown in the figure, these chains are coiled and kinked along their

Figure 25.

(a)

(b)

(c)

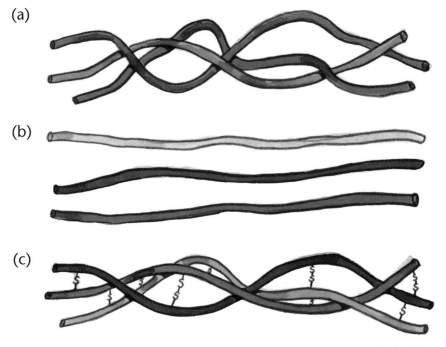

Configurations of rubber chains. a) Natural rubber chains. b) Stretched rubber chains. c) Cross-linked rubber chains.

entire length. When heated and stretched (Figure 25b), the chains elongate and line up. They stay elongated when released. The addition of sulfur to hot rubber changes this because the cross-links form (Figure 25c).

If all the rubber chains are cross-linked, the cross-linked rubber becomes one giant molecule. Such a polymer is impossible to melt because the chains can't slide past each other. It becomes a thermoset. Indeed, most synthetic elastomers burn on heating.

Natural rubber is made mostly of isoprene (see Appendix A) and was the only kind of rubber used until World War II (1939–1945). When the Japanese military seized the plantations that grew the rubber trees, the United States initiated a crash program to develop synthetic rubber. The program was outstandingly successful. Today, there are many different types of rubber that are manufactured for different uses including polybutadiene and styrene-butadiene-styrene (SBS) rubber (see Appendix A).

Elastomers may be formed into different shapes by molding, extruding (pushing through a narrow opening), and foaming, among other ways. In this experiment, you will make a rubber band from *rubber cement* simply by spreading out a few layers of it and allowing the solvent to evaporate. The "rubber" part of the name rubber cement comes from the fact that the product is actually a slow-flowing solution of natural rubber (or, in some brands, synthetic rubber) in a hydrocarbon solvent called hexane (C_6H_{14}). The rubber is intended to be used as an adhesive, but this experiment will take advantage of the fact that the rubber is an elastomer.

Safety: *Read the instructions that are on the container for safe use of rubber cement. The experiment should be carried out in a well-ventilated room. Small* *quantities of rubber cement do not harm the skin, but it is good practice not to allow any solvent on the skin.*

Procedure:

1. Use a pencil and ruler to mark a rectangle about 15 cm (6 in) long by 2.5 cm (1 in) wide on a piece of wax paper.

2. Paint this rectangle with a layer of rubber cement. Allow the rubber cement to dry.

3. Place at least three more layers successively on top of the first, allowing each to dry before painting the next one. Four layers is the minimum needed, although you can add additional layers, if desired.

4. When dry, roll the long side of film with your fingers off the wax paper. You may need to pry the edge of the film free at the start. You will have a thin cylinder of rubber.

5. Stretch it gently to test its elasticity.

6. Lay the rubber on the wax paper in the form of a circle with the ends touching.

7. Place a glob of cement over the two ends to seal them together. When dry, remove your rubber band.

Results and Conclusions

The rubber band that you have made will strengthen a little as the remnant of solvent evaporates. It may not be the most evenly shaped rubber band, but it is a useful one.

You now have all the clues needed to solve the Mysterious Case of Natural Rubber. Why does the vulcanization of natural rubber change it from being sticky at high temperatures and stiff at low temperatures to being rubbery and pliable at high, medium, and low weather temperatures?

Solution to the Mystery

When Goodyear added the sulfur to the rubber with heat, cross-links formed between the chains.

The cross-links did two things. First, they prevented the rubber from stretching too far. Second, the cross-links pulled the stretched chains back to the starting configuration when the rubber was released. The result was that the vulcanized rubber was still an elastomer even in hot weather.

Why did natural rubber become stiff when the weather became cold? That was because cold weather temperatures in Massachusetts were below the T_g of natural rubber. In the cold, the rubber converted to the glassy state and became stiff. Cross-linking changed this. The cross-linking lowered the T_g of the rubber. Hence, vulcanized rubber remained an elastomer even when it got cold.

💡 Science Project Ideas

- What additives are put into synthetic rubber to improve its qualities for different uses? List the additives in a chart with samples of each, and describe their purposes.

- Use rubber cement to make different sizes of rubber bands. Mount them and note how you made them.

- Invent a way to make a rubber band out of rubber cement so that it is formed as a ring without needing to have the ends cemented together.

- Compare the stretchability of a rubber-cement rubber band with a similarly shaped store-bought rubber band. Which breaks first on stretching? Contact the manufacturer to find what causes the difference.

- Investigate the mechanical process by which rubber bands are manufactured for sale. Describe it with diagrams and explanations.

- Demonstrate the elasticity of a rubber balloon by piercing an inflated one with a bamboo skewer without breaking the balloon. The skewers are usually sharp, so be careful with the points. Keep the balloon away from the face in case your demonstration fails and the balloon is popped. Clean off any splinters on the bamboo stick with fine sandpaper before use. Put a light coating of petroleum jelly on the skewer. The best place to insert the skewer is near the tied end of the balloon. Try this same process on a Ziploc bag filled with water. Try it on a paper bag of water. Explain the results.

EXPERIMENT 4.5

Chewing Elastic for Fun

Question:

How much of chewing gum is rubber and how much is sweetener?

Hypothesis:

By chewing the gum or kneading it under water, you can remove the sweetener and leave only the rubber.

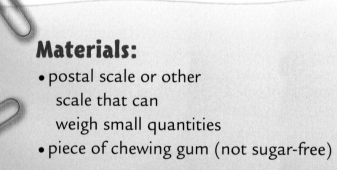

Materials:

- postal scale or other scale that can weigh small quantities
- piece of chewing gum (not sugar-free)

A familiar use of rubber is as an ingredient in chewing gum. Modern chewing gum is made up of six ingredients: a gum base, sugar and corn syrup (or a sugar substitute), softeners to improve the texture of the gum, color, flavors, and a synthetic rubber polymer to make the gum stretchy. The gum base recipe is a mixture of waxes and paraffins (hydrocarbon solids obtained from petroleum) and is a closely guarded secret of the gum manufacturer.

Gums of different kinds were chewed at least as far back as the ancient Greeks, and chewing gums were made in America back in colonial days. Manufactured chewing gum first appeared in the mid-nineteenth century, and bubble gum was first manufactured in 1928. The polymer added to make bubble gum elastic enough to blow into a bubble is a latexlike vinyl rubber.

This rubber was originally made from trees but is now made with the same rubber used for truck tires, namely SBR (styrene-butadiene-rubber). As a result, it can be said that anyone chewing bubble gum is chewing the stuff of truck tires. Although the human stomach can digest a remarkable number of things, it cannot digest rubber. Chewing gums shouldn't be swallowed.

How much of a sample of bubble gum (not the sugar-free kind) is soluble in water, and how much remains in the chewy rubber?

Procedure:

1. Obtain some chewing gum. Weigh a single piece.

3. Place it in your mouth and chew it until the flavor is gone, or knead it under water for a while, testing to see if it still has flavor. How long does it take to lose the flavor?

4. Allow the chewed piece to air-dry. Weigh the dry, chewed piece, being careful to keep it from sticking to the scale you are using. What percentage of the original gum was water-soluble?

Results and Conclusions

Chewing gum must be soft enough to chew easily but strong and flexible enough to be stretched to a thin film. Some of the chemicals added to chewing gum are there to hold down the size of the bubbles. Manufacturers and parents don't want a gum bubble to be larger than a grapefruit, although the largest bubble on record was nearly 60 cm (24 in) in diameter. By incorporating shorter, non-stretchy materials such as waxes, the tendency to break on expansion is increased.

Chewing gum was traditionally made from sweeteners and a natural latex, known as chicle, as the base. However, since rubber is more chewy than chicle and cheaper to manufacture, it is the main ingredient in most modern chewing gum. After the water-soluble natural sweeteners such as sugar, corn syrup, or glucose have been chewed away, what is left is the rubber, or gum, base.

This leftover gum is sticky, of course, and can cause problems if discarded carelessly where it can be stepped or sat upon. Hardened, dried chewing gum can be difficult to remove from clothing or from other undesirable places where it must be manually cleaned off, and it can cause serious damage to electric switches and sensors.

The supermodern Southeast Asian country of Singapore forbids the importation or sale of chewing gum because it had been widely and irresponsibly discarded and became a national nuisance.

💡 Science Project Ideas

- Compare the amount of water-soluble ingredients in sugar-sweetened chewing gum and in artificially sweetened chewing gum. Do the labels show the differences in the ingredients used and the amounts of ingredients? Explain.

- Compare the amount of water-soluble ingredients in sugar-sweetened bubble gum to that of ordinary chewing (not bubble) gum.

- Consider any of the following projects. Find out

  1. which brand of gum has the most gum base

  2. which gum's flavor lasts the longest

  3. which gum has the most intense flavor and how long the flavor lasts

In this book, you have been given a brief introduction to an extensive and fascinating field of chemistry. Plastics make up a vast group of the chemical products of our time, and the uses of plastics are still growing. The next decades will unquestionably produce a great growth in new polymers and plastics. Maybe you will be a part of it. Keep experimenting!

Glossary

chemical bond—A force that holds two atoms together in a particle.

chemical reaction—A process in which one or more substances are changed into other substances by reorganizing which atoms are connected.

chewing gum base—The part of chewing gum that makes it chewy; a mixture of waxes and paraffins (hydrocarbon solids obtained from petroleum).

cross-linked—Referring to adjacent polymer chains that are linked by an atom or groups of atoms.

density—The mass of a material per one volume of it.

elastomer—A highly elastic material that can at least double or triple in length when pulled and can then snap all the way back when released.

gel—A cross-linked polymer that has absorbed a large quantity of solvent.

glass transition temperature—The center of the temperature range at which a polymer changes from hard and brittle (glassy) to pliable and at least slightly elastic (rubbery).

glassy polymer—A hard, brittle polymer; a polymer below its glass transition temperature.

hydrophilic polymer—A polymer with a structure into which water can enter causing it to swell, form a gel, or dissolve.

hydrophobic polymer—A polymer that resists penetration by water.

hypothesis—A guess about what would happen to one variable if a change were made in another variable.

impact strength—A response of a film, usually by stretching or breaking, to an object falling on it under specified conditions.

model—A flat, three-dimensional, or mathematical representation of something that we cannot actually see.

molecule—The smallest bit of neutral matter that can be identified as a specific substance.

monomer—A small molecule that may react chemically to link together with other molecules of the same type to form a polymer.

permeable—Referring to a layer of material that allows something, such as water molecules, to pass through it.

plastic—A material consisting largely of one or more polymers.

polymer—A substance made by linking together at least a thousand of the same repeating segments.

polymer additive—A chemical added to a plastic to alter its properties.

polymer chain—A polymer made up of repeating monomer units attached end to end.

polymer fiber—A long thin strand made from a polymer.

polymer network—Polymer chains that are all connected to each other at various spots.

polymerization—The process by which monomers join together to form polymers.

rubbery polymer—A polymer that gives a little when pressed; a polymer that is above its glass transition temperature.

scientific method—The logical development of a theory based on finding evidence to support it.

solution—A mixture of two or more different substances in which the individual particles of the substances are so intermixed that all parts of the solution are the same.

structural formula—A diagram that shows the kinds and numbers of atoms in a particle and which ones are connected to which other atoms.

tetrahedron—A geometric figure whose four corners are equidistant from the center and are as far from each other as they can get in three-dimensional space.

theory—A logical explanation of a natural observation that is supported by much evidence and that isn't contradicted by any observation.

thermoplastic polymer—A polymer that melts when heated so that it can be molded and shaped and that may be cooled to a solid and then remelted.

thermoset—A polymer that scorches and/or burns without melting first.

variable—A property that can change under given conditions.

vulcanization—A process in which sulfur is added to natural rubber with heat.

Appendix A:

SOME COMMON SYNTHETIC POLYMERS, THEIR MONOMERS, AND APPLICATIONS

Monomer Name	Polymer Name	Uses of Polymer
Butadiene	Polybutadiene	Tires and hoses
Ethylene	Polyethylene	See Appendix B
Ethylene glycol and terephthalic acid	Polyethylene terephthalate (polyester)	See Appendix B
Isoprene	Polyisoprene (same as natural rubber)	Vulcanized products: rubber, rubber cement, waterproof and elastic products
Methyl methacrylate	Polymethyl methacrylate (Lucite, Plexiglas)	Substitute for unbreakable glass and for curved glass
Propylene	Polypropylene	See Appendix B
Styrene	Polystyrene	See Appendix B
Butadiene and styrene	Styrene-butadiene-styrene copolymer (SBS)	Hard rubber for tires, shoes, and other rubber uses where toughness is required
Tetrafluoroethylene	Polytetrafluoroethylene (Teflon)	Lining for pots and metals, piston rings, car bearings, insulation
Vinyl chloride	Polyvinyl chloride	See Appendix B
Vinylidene chloride	Polyvinylidene chloride	Food wrap

Appendix B:
RECYCLING RESIN IDENTIFICATION CODES

Code	Name	Abbreviation	Uses	Recycled Uses
<1>	Polyethylene terephthalate	PETE (PET)	Flexible transparent or opaque containers such as 2-liter soft drink bottles, peanut butter jars, Mylar, fabrics	Laundry bottles, carpeting, fleece
<2>	High density polyethylene	HDPE	Bottles made by blow molding, such as milk, juice, and shampoo bottles; garden furniture; trash cans; pails	Pails, trash cans, toys, pipe, base of soft drink bottles
<3>	Polyvinyl chloride	PVC	Flooring and tile, plumbing pipes, pill bottles, shower curtains, house siding, wire and cable, garden hoses, cooking oil containers, leather-like luggage and upholstery	Usually not recycled
<4>	Low density polyethylene	LDPE	Food wrap, diaper liners, squeeze bottles, bags, container lids	Usually not recycled
<5>	Polypropylene	PP	Indoor-outdoor carpeting, fabrics, packaging, pipes, tents, steering wheels, kitchenware	Usually not recycled
<6>	Polystyrene	PS	Transparent cups, casing for hair dryers and other electrical equipment, Styrofoam for hot cups, egg containers, packing "peanuts," insulated containers	Insulation, plastic wood, pens, and uses that are same as original
<7>	Other		Toothpaste and cosmetic containers, food containers	

Some of the plastics picked up for recycling are used to make chemicals and fuels. Most of those not re-used are incinerated at high temperatures, with air pollution controls during the process. This reduces the bulk by 80 to 90 percent. The incinerated product is sent to landfills.

Further Reading

Bombaugh, Ruth. *Science Fair Success, Revised and Expanded*. Springfield, N.J.: Enslow Publishers, Inc., 1999.

Gardner, Robert. *Science Projects About Kitchen Chemistry*, Berkeley Heights, N.J.: Enslow Publishers, Inc., 2000.

Kerrod, Robin. *New Materials: Present Knowledge, Future Trends*. London: Franklin Watts, 2003.

Knapp, Brian J. *Plastics*. Danbury, Conn.: Grolier, 2003.

Rhatigan, Joe, and Gunter, Veronika. *Cool Chemistry Concoctions: 50 Formulas that Fizz, Foam, Splatter & Ooze*. New York: Lark Books, 2005.

Internet Addresses

American Chemistry Council, Inc. © 2007.
<http://www.americanchemistry.com/Plastics/>

National Geographic Society. *Polymers: They're Everywhere*.
© 1997.
<http://www.nationalgeographic.com/resources/ngo/education/plastics/index.html>

University of Southern Mississippi. *The Macrogalleria: A Cyberwonderland of Polymer Fun*. © 2005.
<http://pslc.ws/macrog.htm>

Index

M

microwave ovens, 135-138

molds or molding process, 64, 66, 146, 157

molecules, 8-9, 18, 22, 35, 43, 46, 50, 54, 61, 76-77, 93, 143

monomers, 9-11, 34-37, 133, 156

N

nylon, 88-91, 133, 143

O

oxygen, 9, 37, 45, 76-77, 81, 87, 96

P

paint, 7, 12-13, 34-39, 71, 86, 131-132

paraffin, 143, 150

permeability, 92-95

Plastic Resin Identification Code, 80, 87, 157

plastics industry, 7-8, 33, 124, 129

plastic wrap, 8, 35, 50, 92-95, 112-116

pollution, 99-100, 157

polybutadiene rubber, 146, 156

polyethylene, 44, 56-58, 92-95, 101, 105-106, 110, 114, 156-157

polyethylene terephthalate (PET), 105, 110, 156-157

polymer chain, 9-11, 19, 35, 40-66, 77, 115, 118, 145

polymerization, 9, 34-39, 71

polymethyl methacrylate, 142, 156

polypropylene (PP), 91, 105, 156-157

polystyrene (PS), 80-86, 105, 109, 118-124, 135-141, 156-157

polyvinyl acetate, 51-53, 131, 142

polyvinyl alcohol (PVA), 55

polyvinyl chloride (PVC), 92-95, 105-108, 114, 156-157

polyvinylidene chloride, 156

R

recycling, 80-82, 99-105, 110-111, 135, 138, 157

rubber, 127-129, 145-156

S

salt, 73-79, 139-140

scientific method, 7, 16-25

silicone, 25, 35

slime, 26, 50-55, 71

sodium polyacrylate, 73-79

styrene-butadiene-rubber (SBR), 151

stretchability, 8-12, 22, 26, 53-54, 95, 112-118, 124, 134, 145-152

styrene-butadiene-styrene rubber (SBS), 146

Styrofoam, 40-41, 46-48, 80-87, 120-124, 157

T

Teflon, 45, 156

thermoplastic polymers, 63-66

thermosets, 63-66

transition temperature, 139-143

V

vulcanization, 129, 148

W

water density test, 104

wax, 99, 123, 143-147, 150-152